THE PROSPEROUS WRITER'S GUIDE TO
MAKING MORE MONEY

Habits, Tactics, and Strategies for Making a Living as a Writer

. . . .

HONORÉE CORDER
BRIAN D. MEEKS

AUTHORS OF *THE NIFTY 15*

ALSO BY BRIAN D. MEEKS (SOMETIMES ARTHUR BYRNE)

Henry Wood Detective series (1-4)

Underwood, Scotch, and Wry

Underwood, Scotch, and Cry

Secret Doors: The Challenge

A Touch to Die For

The Nifty 15

ARTHUR BYRNE

The Magellan Apocalypse series (1-3)

Killing Hemingway

Beautiful Gears

THE PROSPEROUS WRITER'S GUIDE TO
MAKING MORE MONEY

Habits, Tactics, and Strategies for Making a Living as an Author

HONORÉE CORDER
& BRIAN D. MEEKS

Published by Honorée Enterprises Publishing

Copyright 2017 © Honorée Enterprises Publishing

Cover design: Dino Marino ❧ Interior design: 3CsBooks.com

Tradepaper ISBN: 978-0-9980731-6-3
Digital ISBN: 978-0-9980731-5-6

First edition, February 2017

SPECIAL INVITATION

Many like-minded individuals have gathered in an online community to share ideas, render support, and promote accountability. When I first wrote *Prosperity for Writers*, I envisioned helping numerous writers shatter the belief that they must starve to survive. I had no idea what was in store, and the result is an amazing community of 700+ writers, authors, editors, and more!

I'd like to personally invite you to join the The Prosperous Writer Mastermind at HonoreeCorder.com/Writers and Facebook.com/groups/ProsperityforWriters where you will find motivation, daily support, and help with any writing or self-publishing questions.

You can connect with me personally on Twitter @Honoree, or on Facebook.com/Honoree. Thank you so much for your most precious resource, your time. I look forward to connecting and hearing about your book soon!

TABLE OF CONTENTS

INTRODUCTION

We are delighted you're here. We, Brian D. Meeks and Honorée Corder, are prosperous writers.

Brian writes mostly fiction across five genres, under his name and a pen name (Arthur Byrne). He's been at it since January 2, 2010 and makes his living as an author. He enjoys crafting snark with a side order of mockery. Honorée writes nonfiction for business professionals, divorcees, single parents, college-bound students, and, of course, *writers*.

We loved the idea of sharing our knowledge with you, our fellow-writers, so that you, too, could become a full-time (if you so desire), prosperous writer. We hatched the idea of writing a book, this book, so you could take the same journey we've taken: from aspiring full-time writer to actual full-time writer, only in a fraction of the time it has taken us. Part of getting from here to there is getting comfortable with your numbers. Making more money from your writing means understanding your metrics (such as how many books are being sold, how many page reads you're getting if you're enrolled in KDP). It also means understanding how to use math to know if your business is growing, to know how to make it grow faster and easier, and ultimately, to make more money. Oh, and there's one more thing: what to do with your money once you get it! These aspects of the book business aren't as scary or as complicated as you might think.

A Note from Honorée

I'm on record (multiple times) as "hating math." For much of my business life, I avoided looking closely at my numbers for a very long time because I didn't completely understand them. In fact, whenever someone asked me why I chose to pursue goals and coach my clients in 100-day cycles, my answer has *always* been, *I hate math. I don't like to multiply and divide. I want a simple, easy way to keep track of things in my head.* Although it was clearly not enough, all I did was just keep an eye on the bottom line: How much was I making? Was it more than last month? Last quarter? Last year?

You picked up this book because you want to make more money as a writer, right? But already I'm talking about metrics and math. Is this a book about math? Well, yes and no. You see, to make more money, you should not only know how to get it, but you also have to know where to get it—what the best sources are for you. And, once you get it, you need to know what to do with it. While you might be thinking, *I'm pretty sure I know what to do with money when I get it, Honorée,* you might be wrong. Brian and I are going to share some strategies with you in this book that will knock you back in your seat and cause you to behave differently. Which, in turn, will cause you to make more money. But first things first.

Why would someone who is on record as hating math write a book that is, in part, about math? Well, it's all fine and good that I had an aversion to math, but what I didn't know was that it had cost me money. It wasn't until I started paying attention to my metrics (trends, inclinations, and the general direction of my sales) and understanding the math, that my income improved. When I learned the what and the how, I got excited. I realized a few important things:

Metrics and math aren't that difficult, and when I understood them better, I made more money. Just like anything else that at first (second, and fifth) glance seems overwhelming, math is one of those complex concepts that you can grasp easily, if you take it one piece at a time.

Let me say that again: *With an understanding and correct use of metrics and math, I could earn more money.* And without doing more work! What?! Yup, that's right! When you know where to place the fulcrum, you can work the same or less and earn more.

If you're already comfortable with math and metrics, but you just don't like the current results you see, stay with me for a bit longer. There's a lot in here for you, too.

Just like anything you've mastered that once seemed nearly impossible (driving a stick shift or learning a new language, anyone?) opens doorways to new realms, learning not only to understand your metrics and math but also to master them can help you make more money from your writing than you ever thought possible.

When I met the great and wonderful Brian D. Meeks, I was struck by how much he *loves* math. Every single time I say the word math, his response is, *I just love math*. As someone who believes firmly in the power of words of affirmation, I've started saying *I just love math*, too, because you know what? Math is making me more money, and who doesn't love more money? I know, that's why you're here! Embracing math and coming to love it has helped me release my reluctance and embrace the possibilities.

In the event you're ready to return this book from whence it came, I implore you to hang in here! I'm going to take you on a journey, the journey from unconscious incompetence (not knowing what you don't know) to unconscious competence (knowing what you need to know *like a boss*), with Brian guiding us on our path.

Brian is good at math, and he's going to hold your hand, just as he's held mine, and show you how to take the numbers you have and make them as big as you want them to be. He will show you how to read the numbers, how to see where they are going, and (here's the fun and exciting part) how to make the most of them. The two of us together are going to help you maximize your mindset and your money— both directly and indirectly.

What if you could use and understand the numbers you have in such a way that you could increase the "good" numbers, and adjust the "bad" ones? Brian is going to show you everything you need to know, and within the pages of this book, turn you into a math lover, too.

We suggest reading all the way through this book and then start again at the beginning. Take each concept and idea as it comes, learn it and apply it, then continue. What if you're confused or have questions? You're in luck! Brian loves questions, too. We'll tell you in a later section how you can get answers to your questions.

I'm so excited for you to get started, but first, a few words from Brian!

A NOTE FROM BRIAN

I love data. I love math. I love doing math with data a bunch. I, you see, am the son of a mathematician. Dad loves math, too.

If you're cringing because you don't love math, I understand. It didn't come easily to you when you were young, and people tend to gravitate toward the things they do well. It may be tough for me to win the argument that math is cool, considering you've spent your entire life saying (or thinking) how much you hate math every time it comes up, but I'm going to try.

Consider this: remember back in high school when hormones were raging like an ill-tempered mixed martial arts fighter? If you recall, all the pretty girls and handsome guys gravitated toward the kids in math club. Everyone wanted to be cool like the math kids. The players on the football team and the cheerleaders mostly cried themselves to sleep every Friday night because there weren't enough math geniuses to go around.

What? You don't remember it that way? Huh... maybe that's a bad example.

Well, it doesn't matter. What's important is that you'd like to make more money with your books. Honorée and I are going to teach you how to use math and data to do just that. We're going to help point you in the right directions for where and how you can make more money.

What makes me qualified to write about this subject?

I spent seven and a half years as a data analyst with GEICO where a fifteen-minute call could save you 15% on your car insurance. I was in the marketing department, so it was my job to use data and math to find ways to make more money. Also, I have a degree in Economics, which is a lot of algebra, which I love!

What I don't have is a degree in psychology, though I did read an issue of Psychology Today in 1987, so the next bit is based on my vast knowledge of the human psyche.

I'm convinced after thousands of hours of research (or fifteen minutes of thinking about it…give or take) that most people can do most things, and the only barrier holding them back is fear and an abundance of situation-comedies-on-demand through sites like Hulu, Netflix, and Amazon.

I hate feeling stupid, so when I know I should do something, and I'm not sure how, I slip into procrastination mode. Usually, the terrible thing isn't so hard, and I figure it out by asking The Google. For those who hate math, I guess even the simplest math chore can send them into a three-day binge-watching spree to avoid learning how it's done.

For example, if you spent $138 on an advertising campaign, and you had a net revenue of $150 what would your ROI (Return-on-Investment) be?

Some people will know this right away, but mathphobes might say, *I made a profit so who cares?*

The people who want to make offensive amounts of money from their books' sales, that's who.

The reason ROI is important is that it standardizes results, so they are easy to compare. If one has run two hundred ads through a venue like Facebook, Instagram, or Twitter over a period of three months, and they want to up their spend (that's prosperous-writer-speak for "increase how much they are spending on advertising"), being able to compare the results of each advertisement is key.

So, how do you calculate ROI? It's easy, and there are only two bits of information you need. How much did you spend, and how much revenue came in? In the case of Amazon, this is your share of the sale, 70% or 35%. (Yes, I know ROI is really based on how much *additional* revenue came in due to that investment, but you're getting ahead of yourself. We'll cover that in a later chapter. Let's keep it simple for now.)

So, in the previous example, we had a pile of money equal to $150. Now, take your little calculator and subtract the pile of money you spent, $138. You can do that, can't you?

So, there was $12.00 profit. That was easy to find, and nobody died in the process. Now, you simply take the profit and divide it by the first pile of money you spent (invested), which is $138.

Seriously, stop rolling your eyes. Punch 12 into the calculator, hit divide, and then type in 138 and hit the equals button. You'll get 0.08695652. Then, if you just move the decimal point two spots to the right, you'll have 8.69 and then throw one of those fancy pants percent signs on it, and you get 8.69% ROI. (8.7% if you enjoy rounding.)

It doesn't seem like a big number, but what if that ad campaign only ran for one day? What if you could take all the money you got from that ad and put it into an ad the next day and make another 8.7%, what would that be after 90-days?

You'd be trying to figure out how to spend over $190,000 on day 91. That's a good problem to have.

So, if you don't like math, that's fine, but you can still learn a little if it means huge piles of money, can't you?

Remember ROI is the pile of money made minus the pile of money spent, and then that number is divided by the pile of money spent. If you start calculating ROI on things you do, you'll have that formula down far quicker than you'd imagine.

There's one more thing. If you hate math and don't even know your times table up through ten, then learn it. Multiplication is the building block for *everything*, and if you don't know what seven times eight equals in your head, then it's time you learn. Data analysis requires being able to spot things that jump out as "unusual" or "wrong." I'm not kidding; learn it, it's only 100 numbers. Memorize that beast. I'm sure you can even find an app to do it...probably on your eight-year-old's tablet. Don't tell anyone, just learn that table!

Learning these things can mean making a lot of money or avoiding making a decision that will cost you a bunch.

Now, let's get to the fun stuff.

1

CLARITY IS POWER

Before we dive into the *how-tos* of making more money as a writer, there are probably a few things we should clear up about us. Also, there are several areas in which you need to gain clarity that will help you in your pursuit of more cash.

As full-time writers with a full two decades of experience between us in the author business, we've learned a lot of things we wish we'd known sooner—like the day before we started. While there's no return button for us to press to send ourselves back in time while still holding onto all our knowledge, we know our combined experience can catapult you from the rocky road of unpredictable results to the newly paved eight-lane highway of monetary author success.

We love the author business! And there are a few reasons why. Not the least of which is, as Kevin Tumlinson (author of *30-Day Author*) would say: "*Pants are optional.*" Seriously, we can't think of one thing we don't love about writing and about our author businesses. Part of the reason we are so happy is that we got clear on a few things we think you should be clear about, too.

WHAT'S YOUR WHY?

Let's start with why. We believe most writers write because they are compelled to write. Very simply, we write because we must. But that's not the only *why*, is it? Nope. Without question, we know you're here reading a book about making more money as a writer because you want to make more money as a writer. But *why?* Not because, or not only because, you have some bills to pay, although that could be a big reason. You can even add "pay my bills" to your *why* list. But in addition to the more general why, we suggest you get clear on your very deep personal *whys*.

Without going too deep down the self-help rabbit hole, without an unyielding *why*, you may be tempted to abandon the writing ship when the sailing gets rough. When it's been too long between freelance gigs, or Amazon changes its price per page read, or you publish a new book and seemingly do everything right, only to have it languish in obscurity you might be tempted to give up. We know, we've been there ourselves.

On the other hand, a strong *why* is going to get you up early and keep you up late. A solid *why* is going to help you say *yes* to writing and *no* to other things, when the other things are darned tempting and or very sexy. So, before you read any further, grab your journal or start a new document in Evernote and jot down why you are writing. Next, write why you must make more money from your writing.

Did you get that down? If not, and you're just still reading along, do yourself and your income a favor and just do it! It'll just take a couple of minutes, and we promise those couple of minutes are well spent.

All set? Great, keep that journal or document handy, and let's continue!

Who's Who?

The next bit of clarity that will be most helpful to you is to get clear on your *who*. Who are you as a writer? More specifically, who are you as a full on, money-making writer? Yep, we are going to suggest you write those down too. Next, for whom are you writing? No, not your kids, not *that* kind of *who*. We have something different in mind, or more to the point, someone. The someone could be the editor of *The New York Times*. Or, the someone could be the middle-aged Midwestern housewife who delights in reading a knotty romance every afternoon before the kids come home from school. The person you have in your mind is your avatar, also known as your *who*.

Knowing whom you're writing for will help you to make those tricky writing decisions (Which way should the story go? What information should I include in my book?), will help keep you focused, and frankly, will help make writing a whole heck of a lot easier for you.

We suggest taking five to ten minutes and jot down your *who*. When you're done, keep reading.

WAIT, WHAT?

Next, let's talk about *what* you write. Some people only want to write what they love to write. Some people believe they should write what they don't love to write, if they want to make money. We believe you can do both: identify what you can write that people will love to read (also known as what people will *pay* to read). This is called "writing to market." Chris Fox recently wrote a book aptly titled *Write to Market*, and in it he discusses that somewhat controversial approach to writing. But let's face it, you're not just a writer; you're a business person. Every legitimate business is based on supply and demand, including your very own book business. Writing of every kind is no different. It will behoove you and your bank account to spend some time in serious, contemplative thought before you write. Before you market your services or skills, figure out how to cross the intersection of what you love to write and how you can earn a profit and/or a living from it.

We suggest starting with *What do I love to write?* Whether you write fiction or non-fiction, to be successful and make (more) money as a writer, you'll have to write *a lot*. So, you've got to love what you write. Otherwise, you not only won't want to do it, eventually, you won't do it. Yes, even doing what you love can be categorized as work. For some of us, it's as close as we'll get to a job, and even still, writing is work. Sorry if that feels like a bucket of ice water over your head right there, but it's true. No matter how much you love writing, it is work. It makes sense, then, that you should love what you're writing, in order to rig things as much as possible in your favor.

Having said all of that, if what you love to write is of zero interest to anyone, you won't sell your writing. Enter the concept of "write to market." As we've mentioned, Chris Fox wrote an excellent book about this, and we agree with just about everything he says on the subject. The business of being an author requires forethought, planning, and strategy. The planning and strategy piece is where some writers get stuck, and here is a thought to help: every piece of writing requires readers who want to buy it and read it. To that end, you'll want to do some thinking before putting pen to paper or fingers to keyboard. Ask yourself, *What's in it for my reader?* Every writer has people around them cheering them on, and some of those people are relying on said writer to earn a living from writing so they can do important things like eat, put gas in the car, pay the mortgage, and so on. *What's in it for the ones you love?*

Please take a moment and jot down your thoughts.

WHERE ARE YOU GOING TO WRITE?

Next is *Where am I going to write?* If you're Mark Dawson, before he left his day job as an attorney in London, you write on the train or bus during your commute. If you're Honorée, you write whenever and wherever you can. She prefers an especially comfy spot on her couch, but can come up with words in a back bedroom at her mother-in-law's house, at any coffee shop worldwide, and even, occasionally, by a hotel pool. Just yesterday, she knocked out some words on her iPad (using Dragon Anywhere and her shiny new Logitech keyboard) in front of the elevators at the Four Seasons in Austin while waiting for a meeting to start. Brian cranks out words in his fully-appointed writing den/writing haven and has been known to manage a few words in-between crushing opponents on the tennis court.

Point being, you can write anywhere. You must have the belief you can. Make a short list of *where* you prefer to write your words *and write them on schedule* (we'll talk about that in a moment). But when life gets in the way, you are at this moment given permission to create your masterpiece wherever you happen to find yourself.

WHEN IN ROME (OR WHENEVER)

Finally, *When will I find the time* is almost every aspiring writer's objection. We don't believe you "find" it; we believe you "make" it. Honorée's writing sprint earlier this week was just after her morning practice, before jumping in the shower, and before working with a client all day. She had just enough time to squeeze in about 800 words in 15 minutes. She has a recurring 6 a.m. appointment to write, and we suggest you create a recurring appointment in your calendar. If your current schedule is somewhat set in stone, and you can predict when you'll have availability, this will work well for you. If your schedule is somewhat or totally unpredictable, block out times for writing on your calendar at least a day, and ideally a week, beforehand. When you treat your writing as an immovable commitment, a non-negotiable appointment you have with yourself, you will write. And therefore, you will make more money from writing! You may want to check out our book in *The Prosperous Writer Series: The Nifty 15: Write Your Book in Just 15 Minutes a Day*, which talks in detail about these ideas.

Consider this: What gets your attention and focus is what you deem important. We're sure you can agree that what is considered important is what gets done. Your writing is a business, and we're going to dive into the nooks and crannies of making more money in upcoming chapters, but first it's important you understand that you are not only a writer and an artist, but you are also a businessperson. Your writing business will require you to put it at the top of your list of priorities. You can, and you must, not only write, you must work on your mental settings, take control of your calendar, and learn to do the other critical activities that are a part of a successful writing business.

Now that you've gotten a handle on some of the basics of making more money as a writer and gained much-needed clarity, let's explore some of the other exciting and crucial factors that will contribute to you making, earning, and attracting more of the green stuff.

Let's do this, shall we?

2

WHAT'S MATH GOT TO DO WITH IT?

We're artists, creators, and writers, right? Worrying about "math" or "data" isn't something we've wanted to think about, nor been encouraged to think about (or learn about). As a matter of fact, artists are known by two underlying stereotypes: they are poor, and they aren't business people. As we suggested in the first chapter, we believe these assumptions are wrong. Especially today, with the climate weighted heavily in favor of the aspiring full-time writer, this book is going to show you why those assumptions are wrong and how to understand and use math to your highest advantage.

Now when Honorée mentioned this book to a fellow writer (who shall remain nameless, but you know who you are!), that writer scrunched up her face and said, *No math! I hate math!* To which Honorée replied, and Brian was proud, *I used to hate math, too, but now that I understand it, I love it.*

Of course, we use numbers for everything, every day, in all sorts of ways, from how many multivitamins to take to how many cups (pots?) of coffee you need before you can get going. We even use math to calculate how many words we've written versus how many more we need to write. Right? Of course, if just thinking about math or calculating nearly anything gets you about as excited as finding a spider in your shoe, it really shouldn't. And, if you go all the way through this book with an open mind, it won't. You'll realize you can use all numbers to your advantage. Like Honorée, after a bit of time, you quite possibly could be won over and be heard to say, *I love math!* (and mean it).

The first step in upping your comfort level and learning to love the numbers is understanding the various terms, how they're used, and what they mean.

(Please note: if you have a math degree, this section isn't for you.)

We all know what math is, but data can be a small word that strikes fear based on our lack of understanding. When most people talk about data, they mean numbers: metrics (how many books have sold thus far), math (adding, subtracting, multiplying, and dividing to gain clarity), and money (the result of your efforts). When Brian says "data" he does *not* mean metrics, math, and money. Data is just a term that means pieces of information in their rawest form. We'll get into this in depth in the next chapter, but here's a quick example. If you had two days of sales of seven units and ten units, respectively, that would total seventeen units. You would consider the numbers 7 and 10 to be data, but not the number 17, because we arrived at that number through a formula (Day 1 + Day 2). Furthermore, if the seven units and ten units were a sum of the sales for three different titles, then the 7 and 10 wouldn't be data either; the individual book sales numbers would be the data.

Understanding data is important because as your business grows, you'll want to maintain data at the most fine-grained level possible. The data should be kept in their own sheet and referenced through formulas. This gives you the most flexibility when it comes to analyzing your data.

Metrics are the summary, average, mean, ROI (return on investment), and more, of a specific data set. Total sales equal all the sales for a period, be it a day, week, or month. We want to have the sales at the daily level, and then we can create formulas to give us the week or month.

As you can see, math has everything to do with your success as a writer, so it's high time you knew all about it!

3

THE BASICS

The basics include lots of words you have probably associated with math and therefore you may have shied away from them. But imagine Honorée's delight when Brian used the very words she thought were beyond her comprehension to help get more of what she wants? While she wasn't excited about *math* (initially), she was excited to learn how understanding the numbers could help her predict trends, adjust her marketing strategies, and ultimately, make more money. We both think you'll find your delight, too. And, it won't be difficult at all!

This is Honorée, and I'm going to hand it over to Brian to walk you through this part (while reserving the option to interject at any moment).

Let's start with that doozy of a math word: data.

Data

Looking at data, which is the most fun thing in the world, is a bit of an art.

Oh, I hear you chuckling. You don't think it's fun to look at a bunch of numbers in a spreadsheet, but you will, once you realize it is like looking for treasure. Everyone likes treasure.

The way one finds treasure is to notice a pattern that other people haven't seen. Some patterns can be helpful in improving sales. We want to teach you what sort of pattern to look for in your data.

As an example, if you have been running a bunch of Facebook ads—let's say twenty—you're going to have some ads that outperform the others. Assuming that it's just random luck isn't helpful, so it's worthwhile to see if you can find something similar in the ads that might be making them do so well.

I have one bit of ad copy for my satire, *Underwood, Scotch, and Wry,* that I wrote just because it made me laugh. I had no idea if it would perform well or not. This copy has crushed it! I mean super-duper, call-Mom, run-around-the-house-dancing, crushed it. The ROI on this ad varied from day to day between 600% and 800%, which is massive. I had never had another ad come even close to that.

Naturally, I tried some other silly ads. They did fine but were less productive in their results.

Patterns and Trends

You're probably curious what my ad copy was. It's a secret…so don't tell anyone…only you and the hundreds of thousands of people who saw the ad know about it.

"More snark than a snark-o-potumus in Snark Town on a snarking spree."

It's completely ridiculous, but so is making 800% ROI. A month later, I was writing an ad for my science fiction series, and I included the phrase "…with just a bit of snark." Guess what? It was my best science fiction ad. It didn't do as well as the one for the satire, but it did beat all the other ads for those books.

That's what we call a repeating theme in the data. It isn't enough data to be considered statistically significant, but it is enough to form a hypothesis: *people like the word "snark,"* and then to test it.

In fact, there are lots of words that will give one a better chance of getting that person to click. The words will change over time and vary by genre, but some will be more powerful than others. If you can figure out the ones that work for your book, it will be your own pirate gold.

A close cousin to patterns are trends. A **trend** is simply the direction that things are moving. If your sales are trending upwards, it might be beneficial to know why. If they're trending downward, it might be crucial to uncover the culprit.

The thing about trends is they can be hard to spot with daily data because book sales can vary so much from day to day. Two years ago, I was happy every day I got a sale. When I ran a promotion, there would be a huge spike. No mystery there, I spent money on a platform that advertises discounted books, and some people bought. Typically, a book that would have one to three sales per day at full price would have 100 to 200 for a day at 99 cents.

As my readership grew, and I started to get five to ten sales per day on a consistent basis I had enough data to look for trends. Still, the jumping around of the numbers—3, 7, 1, 1, 8, 5—made it hard to tell what was happening. We begin to understand what is happening by calculating a moving average.

THE MOVING AVERAGE

A moving average is a *very* useful thing to know about. It can be used to track trends for sales or ad spend, as both are valuable metrics to track. Again, thinking about running Facebook ads, one would likely see their daily spend jump around just like the sale because some days' ads deliver more clicks than others. If you know your ad dollars are returning a positive ROI (you're finding treasure), then it would be good to spend even more money, because more doubloons await.

Your daily spend and a seven-day moving average of your spend are both valuable metrics to keep an eye on. To calculate a seven-day average simply total up the spend for 7 days and divide by, wait for it, 6.9 (no, just kidding, it's 7). To do a moving average one simply adds the new day to the total and removes the day that is now eight days prior.

It's a pain to do on paper but super easy on Excel. I'll teach you how later.

The point is, with a moving average, you smooth out the bumps. The longer the moving average, the smoother the data, so you could do 14-days, 30-days, or even longer, but one can also have such a long range that it flattens out the line so much that it's useless. I like seven days.

19

Another fun thing to watch for are **records**. A record is the best day at anything, be it highest sales, highest point on a moving average, most spent, or the high point of any other bit of data you might be tracking. If you are continually getting new "best net profit" days, then you're doing something right. If you haven't set a record in eight months, well, you may be playing too many video games.

These are some of the basics. There are many other measurements one can calculate with Excel that are valuable, but I don't want to scare you. Okay…maybe just one more.

Pearson's Strength of Correlation

When I was a data analyst at GEICO, I used to like to calculate Pearson's strength of correlation for my customer retention data. A simple example might be *If I spend more money on ads, will I make more money?*

On the surface, it seems like the answer is always *yes*, but that assumes that your current advertising plan is scalable without any drop-off in results. A Pearson's strength of correlation is just a way of describing how close a relationship there is between two sets of numbers. If you have a bunch of data points where you've been increasing your spend and tracking how much money came in, you'll be able to use Excel (or your favorite spreadsheet such Google Sheets or Numbers) as to see how strong the correlation is between spending money and making profits.

Pearson's returns a number between −1 and 1. If the result is close to zero, then there isn't any correlation between the two things you're comparing. If it is closer to 1 or -1, then there is a strong correlation (either positive or negative). The stronger the correlation, the more likely it is that there is a strong relationship between increasing your ad spend and increasing your profit.

There are lots of high-level statistical tests one can do, but for the most part, they're overkill for what we're trying to accomplish, which is sell more books. If one were trying to improve the bottom line at Random House (or any of the large New York Publishing houses) and looking at their entire catalog, those other measurements might be more useful.

The point is you can do just a little or get really fired up and do a bunch. Regardless, the better you get at seeing stuff in your data the better your chance of building a sustainable career as an author.

Are you with me so far? Good! If not, go here to get weekly updates and connect with the authors here HonoreeCorder.com/Writers. Now, let's continue.

DATA ANALYSIS IS ABOUT ASKING AND ANSWERING QUESTIONS

The hardest part of data analysis isn't the math because one can set up Excel to do that. The trickiest part about data is knowing what questions to ask, and asking those right questions.

Thinking of data questions is a skill just like anything else. The more you train yourself always to be wondering, the easier it becomes. When I run a promotion, and look at the data, curiosity sets in, and the questions pop into my head.

If my book's ad went out in an email blast and was the third of six books listed in the blast, I wonder if there would have been more downloads (or sales) if it had been first.

One doesn't always need to analyze the data to draw intuitive and self-evident conclusions, either. Just considering how people behave, when one thinks about an enormous group, it's easy to imagine that being first on the email blast would be best.

A portion of the people who open the email will choose to click on the first book. Some percentage of those people will purchase and download the book. And of those who do, some will begin reading right away and never return to the email.

I don't need to know if it is 5% or 20% for this thought exercise to be valuable. When dealing with a large set of data (in the case of BookBub mystery genre, over 3.5 million readers), the knowledge that nearer the top is better than being sixth is enough.

But Brian, we don't have control over where the book runs?

No, we don't, but when comparing two ads that ran six months apart, knowing where the book was in the email could be valuable in understanding differences between the two ads with regards to their performance.

This is just one example of how to consider future events so that one might continually gather a greater understanding of their business.

What are some other questions that I might want to ask myself?

In author forums, one sees the same questions over and over, and those are a good place to start.

Is XYZBooks.com a good place to advertise my epic guinea pig fantasy series and is $25 to reach 50,000 readers a good rate?

I'm running a countdown deal on my book, 25 signs your imaginary boyfriend is cheating on you, and I was wondering how many days I should run it?

In the first month of my cross-genre (Romance/ Motorcycle Death Race) novel, I've averaged five sales per day, is that good?

Knowing the answers to these questions can make a huge impact on one's bottom line. ("Bottom line" is prosperous writer-speak for how much profit you make, not the concluding sentence of your novel.)

But Brian, isn't focusing on making money evil? Doesn't that mean you're a terrible person who's greedy, wants to destroy the planet, and see orphans starve to death in the streets ravaged by war and famine?

No. Money isn't inherently evil or good; it is simply a medium of exchange. If you've written a story about puppies and penguins battling an ill-tempered mongoose, and people decide they want to exchange their money for your book, then money has done nothing wrong. In fact, it has made the smiles you brought to the readers' faces possible.

Furthermore, ebooks don't require any deforestation, so by selling a portion of your books in non-paper form you're saving the planet. Well done!

As for war and famine, if people are shooting guns, it cuts into their reading time, and I hate being hungry. I love snacks.

And those pesky orphans? Well, if you make a bunch of money, you can donate dozens of Xboxes to them so they keep off the streets, which may or may not be war-ravaged. Nothing keeps an orphan off a war-torn street like a first-person shooter game.

So, in summary, you've been given permission to make a metric boatload of money, if for no other reason than to develop superior gaming skills among the orphan set.

Let's continue.

4

READING THE NUMBERS

Now that you have a basic understanding of the numbers and hopefully have overcome any resistance you have to them, you're ready for the next level. Seeing numbers and being able to read them (and know what they mean) will allow you to do lots of things. Cool things, such as spotting trends, making predictions, and even adjusting what you're doing or not doing—we're talking about marketing, production, and other types of planning. Which all eventually lead to—yup, you guessed it—making more money.

Reading and understanding the numbers is obviously Brian's area of expertise, so he's going to take it from here.

How Can Numbers Help You?

There are so many things we can learn from asking questions of our numbers and making sense of the data. It's the questions that then lead to a better understanding of the book business world, and the ones who have that understanding are at a huge competitive advantage to those who are just guessing their way through.

Case Study: Advertising Venues Change

In 2013, there was a place one could advertise their books when they were on sale for 99 cents that did well for me. They charged 25% of the net profit (which they tracked through their affiliate link) so no matter how many books you sold you were in the black.

I had run three ads through them for three different books in my mystery series, and all three had yielded around 200 sales. My profit on a 99-cent book was 35 cents, after Amazon got their cut. $200 \times 0.35 = \$70$. The advertising venue took 25% of that ($17.50) which left me with $52.50.

The ads got me new readers, some of whom would go on to read other books of mine, so the actual profit from the ads was even better than the $103.50.

I had dozens of author friends who all used this service and had similar results. The venue had over a half-million followers on Facebook, and they could move the needle. In fact, we all considered this venue to be the best one beyond BookBub.

The first week of December 2013, the ads running on this site stopped working.

It was baffling to all of my author friends. They would run an ad, and it would fail to deliver even 10% of what their previous ads had done. Then they would try another. Now, they didn't lose money because of the 25% rule, but they also didn't have any idea why.

Soon, this venue changed their policy and went to a flat fee model. The sudden downturn in the effectiveness of the ads had wiped out their revenue stream.

This is where it's important to understand the "*why*" of it all. For the authors who hadn't used this venue in a while, they had no idea they had lost their effectiveness and gladly paid the flat fee only to lose money. For the authors who had noticed a low performing ad or two, but chalked it up to "bad luck" or "day of the week" or some other theory unsupported by data, they kept pouring their money into ads hoping it would get back to the way it was before.

I knew immediately what the problem was because I think like a data person. I knew that this venue relied on the people who followed their Facebook page, and I read a lot of blogs about the state of social media. The first week in December 2013, Facebook all but killed organic reach for posts.

Before Facebook's change, a post to the venue's page (which was the "advertisement") would reach around 40% of the over half-million people who had "liked" this venue's Facebook page, or around 200,000 people. Overnight that number of people reached dropped to less than 10,000 people. You don't need to be a data guru to see the problem when you understand what's going on behind the scenes.

The venue was dead in the water, and there wasn't an easy solution. They have since worked hard to shift their fans to an email list, but it is a slow process. It is far more difficult to get someone to subscribe to a list than it is to hit "like" on a page.

I never ran an ad with them after the first week in December because I had a theory it would be ineffective. I verified the theory by talking to other authors about their results. My understanding of my past data (and that of other authors) and the current state of affairs with Facebook saved me from spending money on ads that wouldn't have had a positive ROI.

Not losing money is as important as making money when it comes to advertising.

How to Use the Numbers to Make Decisions, or Danger: Erroneous Conclusions can be Expensive

It's important to understand the difference between hypothesis and reliable theory. If one has an idea for something that might increase sales, and they try it once, and it does, that doesn't mean they have an established theory; it means they have one successful test.

Be careful when making massive changes to your business based on incomplete data.

Case Study: CPC Giddiness Gone Awry

Some advertising venues (for example, Facebook and Instagram) allow one to run ads on a cost-per-click (CPC) basis, where the advertiser pays each time someone clicks on the ad. They also allow one to run ads on a cost-per-thousand (CPM, the "M" is Latin number equivalent for 1,000) basis, where the person advertising (you) is charged for every 1,000 impressions, or every time the ad is shown to 1,000 people. These are the two basic models for running ads on these venues.

In one instance, another author friend of mine and I were testing out some strategies. We were using the CPC model and bidding how much we would be willing to pay for clicks. If one bids too low, then the ad won't get shown to anyone because there is someone else bidding more and Facebook will choose to show that ad.

I had been running my test for a couple of months and learning all sorts of interesting things. My friend decided he wanted to give it a go, too. He writes in a different genre from the five I write in, so we both knew that my data wouldn't necessarily translate into how he should bid.

After trying a couple of ads for a few days using my bids, he decided to increase his bid because he wasn't getting any impressions. That's a reasonable thing to do. He started to get impressions and stayed with the higher bid. This means that every time someone clicks on his ads he is spending more than if they clicked on mine, but it seemed it was necessary.

As is sometimes the case, advertising venues change or get more competitive, and this seemed to be happening to us. Our impressions for our ads dropped considerably over a four-week period.

We both decided that we had plenty of margin and increasing the bid some would be reasonable. I increased the bid on about 30% of my ads, leaving the other 70% as the control group. I made sure that I had some ads from each of my books at both the new and old bids.

My friend did the same thing, for a few days.

He immediately saw a huge spike in impressions and decided to change all of his ads.

He is now spending more per click, and that's cutting into his margin. But if it's generating more impressions as a result, then that's a smart move.

Here's the problem: he didn't have enough data.

I left mine just the way they were for about a month. At the end of that time I had seen some ads with incredible spikes in impressions, but here is the important part, I saw them in both groups (old bid and new bid).

With four weeks of data, I concluded that the increase in our bids had zero impact on the number of impressions that were being delivered. The ads that were at the old, lower, bid had just as likely a chance of catching fire as the ads with the higher bid and lower profit margin.

The conclusion is that there was something else going on at the venue that was causing the fluctuation in impressions (which leads to clicks), and though we didn't know what it was, we did know that spending more per click wasn't helping.

If I had changed all my ads, I might have drawn the same conclusion as my friend and ended up staying at that higher bid well into the future. This would have eaten up a lot of my profits without being necessary at all.

Jumping to conclusions is easy to do. I've seen this countless times in forums of people who are working on Facebook ads. They try an ad for three days and conclude it is doing well or awful. I would bet that 95% of new advertisers on Facebook decide if an ad is working within 72-hours of its approval. Those people then make decisions based on that limited data.

I consider all the data from the first seven days to be questionable. I never make decisions based upon the early results for several reasons.

1. I don't know if there is a lag in the reporting of impressions, clicks, and spend. Often there *is* a lag, and if this is the case, one needs to

compare results from Wednesday with sales from Monday. Assuming that the reporting data are always real-time is foolish, even if sometimes it's pretty close.

2. Some ads don't get queued up to start running, even if they've been approved, for a few days (or sometimes a few weeks). If an ad isn't generating any impressions the first three days, that doesn't mean it doesn't work. I've had ads that started generating impressions some time between day seven and twenty-one and then turned out to be rather effective. If an ad isn't yielding impressions it doesn't cost you anything, so why not let it sit for a while? Many authors are too quick to terminate ads that don't work.

3. Different days of the week matter. I want to see how an ad does across several weeks to get a true feel for its potential.

It should be noted that once an ad is generating clicks, it's costing you money and being patient when an ad seems to be generating little return can be hard. Each person must find their threshold for pain. That being said, though, at the very least don't be too quick to pull ads that are just sitting there doing nothing, because they do not cost you a dime.

BEWARE OF FALSE SIGNS

Once your mind has started to think like a data analyst, you may accidentally start to draw inferences that lead to erroneous conclusions.

I don't always see the forest for the trees. Despite loving data and training myself to look for opportunities, I still missed a great opportunity.

It cost me $60,000 over the last twelve months.

My blind spot was the book description. I hated writing them. They were always the last thing I did before hitting publish because I found the process mentally painful. Writing a 50,000-word novel was a breeze by comparison to a 300-word description.

Writing descriptions is worse than peas.

The mere thought of trying to improve my description made me shudder. One day, though, my little voice said, "You've spent countless hours analyzing your advertising copy and found that conversion improves with better copy. Why wouldn't it be the same with your description?"

I told my little voice, "Piss off."

My little voice is used to me ignoring it and kept at me. Eventually, I had to consider the value of copywriting and the fact that I am *not* a trained copywriter.

This meant one thing. I had to learn about the art of copywriting or hire a proper copywriter. For most people, it may be a smart financial move to spend the money for a professional, but part of the reason I like to learn things myself is for the data.

I knew I'd want to run tests and the thought of waiting on someone else to get the next bit of copy done just didn't work for me. I dropped everything and started to read up on the art of copywriting.

The first book was the *Adweek Copywriting Handbook*, which I can't recommend enough. It's based on Joseph Sugarman's seminars from the seventies and deals with print ads mostly, but the premise is the same.

The first thing I learned changed my life.

Before I get to that, though, I want to mention a common problem among most authors. We (myself included) tend to think that there is one type of reader who is identical to us. I, personally, rarely ever read the description of a book, or look inside. I read the reviews, instead, and usually quite a few of them.

If all readers were like me, then the description wouldn't have any bearing on sales. Fortunately for humanity, all readers aren't middle-aged, angst-ridden, men with an unhealthy loathing of fruit in Jell-O.

And all readers aren't like you.

We authors make far too many decisions based on our gut. Our gut doesn't have much data and only cares about the next time it's going to get bacon. It can't be trusted.

The cure for this mindset is to imagine one million people of all ages, races, tastes, and hair styles. Just because you don't ever click on an author profile before deciding to give a book a try, doesn't mean that nobody does. In fact, we can assume that some portion of the one million people do click on the link. Perhaps they are interested in finding a new author to love and don't want to buy just one book; they want to find a series to while away the hours.

If you are super price-conscious, it doesn't mean that everyone is going to be the same. In that group of one million readers, a portion of them don't care if a book is $4.99 or $6.99. They'll buy the book they want regardless.

I know, I've gotten a little off track since I almost mentioned the bit of copywriting advice that changed my life, but it's important. You need to understand that there are hundreds of decisions we need to make as authors, and your gut is going to try to chime in on all of them.

One bit of logic that can lead a person astray and seems logical is "This best seller's description is short, so that must be the way to get a lot of sales. Keep it short and sweet because nobody reads those things anyway."

I want you to hear your inner voice when it's making those sorts of proclamations and ask it, "Where's your data?"

There are a multitude of factors that go into a book becoming a best seller. Maybe that author had a friend who knew Bill Gates and recommended the book to him. Maybe Bill sent out a tweet that he loved it, and the book took off from there. Maybe it didn't matter that the description was crap.

That's my point. Try not to jump to conclusions based upon the first thing that pops into your mind.

Now, about that life changing bit of ad copy advice.

The point of everything in the copy is to do one thing…get the reader to read the first line.

It has been proven that most people when confronted with a piece of advertising copy, be it in an email, magazine, or book description, scan the copy to decide if it is worth their time.

They look for clues that the copy may have something they need or want. So, a clever copywriter will have headlines in bold, bullet points, and short easy to read sentences throughout. If they are done right, then the potential customer will go back to the beginning and truly read the first line.

Take a moment and think about this.

Are you familiar with the term "click-bait?" Of course you are, and the reason is that we've all been tricked by "You won't believe what these stars said about their famous exes!"

If it makes you click, even though you know you're being sucked in, it's good copy.

But Brian, I don't want to trick people into buying my book.

I don't want you to trick them to buy your book, either, I want you to trick them into reading the description. There is a big difference.

After I had finished reading *Ad Week*, I went to work on my descriptions.

The first thing I noticed surprised me to no end.

Before I get to that, though, let me remind you, I'm a data person. I'm also tricky. I knew from my data that when I drove people to my book on Amazon, they converted from viewing the book information to purchasing it at a rate between 1 in 20 and 1 in 30. Where I became blind was that I assumed that was the best that could be done. For a year, I drove traffic to my books with descriptions that were poorly written and converting poorly.

Did I mention that I'm tricky?

Why, yes you did. What did you mean by that?

Three times in this chapter I've used a copywriting technique called an "open loop." The last one was just above when I wrote, "The first thing I noticed surprised me to no end." That's an example of a headline that's designed to get the reader to move on because they're curious as to what the thing I noticed was. It's an open loop because I went off on a tangent to introduce the reader (you) to an important point before we get to the answer (closing the loop).

That's why I'm tricky.

The one thing I learned was that now that I had a basic understanding of copywriting technique, the task that I had hated in the book business more than any other, was now something I wanted to do.

Yes, I went from hate to love.

I was excited because I now had a change I could make and measure. If you recall, earlier I mentioned that when I drove people to my book on Amazon, they converted at a rate between 1 in 20 and 1 in 30. This was after I had added: "Praise for..." at the top of some of my descriptions and seen a measurable increase in conversions.

So, what could I do if I wrote a solid headline, used shorter sentences, and focused on truly moving the reader from one line to the next?

The answer is: **Make a Bunch More Money**.

OLD Version

Mitch is facing the real possibility that the woman of his dreams may actually feel the same way about him. He's in love and blissfully unaware of the man who has been following him, a man willing to pin a string of murders on him in the name of revenge.

The murders begin in Italy. Alexis Liao, a former FBI agent, is brought in to consult on the case. After two bodies are discovered, both with the same ATM mark, she knows they have a serial killer on their hands. There are just two problems, no reasonable suspects, and after the first two victims, the bodies stop coming.

NEW Version

Praise for *A Touch To Die For*

"I could hardly put the story down." "The plot is too brilliant to even try to relate, and the characters...unique. Worth the read." "Loved the characters and story line"

Mitch had no idea he was being watched.

For decades, Paul couldn't let it go. The personal slight pecked at his brain just before the quiet of sleep arrived. It fueled his hate. Money, success, and fame almost got him past it—until he saw his nemesis, Mitch, with that beautiful woman.

Mitch couldn't believe he was finally with her. A lifetime of distant longing had faded and turned into joy. The scales of happiness finally tipped in his favor. He thought nothing could ruin his day.

He was wrong.

Paul knew that killing Mitch wouldn't satisfy his lust for vengeance. He needed more. He needed something that would devastate Mitch to the core and last for the rest of his life. Paul would make Mitch a murderer. Better yet, he would make the world *believe* that their beloved author was a deranged serial killer.

Who will win?

Who will survive?

You won't believe the twists and turns in this suspense thriller.

Pick up your copy with just one click.

How did you decide to dip your toes into the suspense and thriller genre?

I had just finished the fourth book in my Henry Wood Detective mystery series and was ready to begin a new novel. The problem was I didn't know yet what Book Five in the series would be about. I know that when I shop for something to read I love looking not only for mystery bestsellers, but also for suspense thrillers, and I decided that a psychological thriller might be fun to write.

Where did you get the idea for your first thriller Kindle book?

The books I enjoy in the thriller genre always make me ask at least one question. In *A Touch To Die For* I wanted to explore what it might be like for a genius to evolve into a serial killer. All the serial killers I can remember are geniuses who seem to know every detail about how to get away with murder. Surely there must have been a learning curve?

What type of reader would enjoy your brand of suspense novel?

My writing tends to be character-driven. I especially like character interaction and am interested in their dialog back and forth. I think I get that from my love of Elmore Leonard. Readers who enjoy clever banter with a side of humor will like *A Touch to Die For*.

This change, which admittedly took several hours to write, pushed my conversions to between 1 in 6 and 1 in 12, with most days being closer to 1 in 6.

Because I have tons of historical data, I went back and calculated how much I had left on the table by not doing this back when I made the "Praise for…" change. It came out to approximately $60,000.

Do you see what I did there?

That was my first open loop, and I just closed it. I hinted at the $60,000 earlier and just now explained why that was the case.

Don't cry for me, Argentina. I'm doing just fine, and that missed opportunity didn't make me sad at all. In truth, it was quite the opposite. I was thankful that I figured out the error of my ways after only twelve months. Can you imagine how much more it would have cost me if I had waited five more years and twenty more books?

You'll drive yourself crazy if you dwell on the past instead of rejoicing in the future. My sales are better now because of the new conversion. Because I'm converting better, my books are staying ranked on the various lists longer, which means more organic eyeballs.

It's all part of the process.

There's another point to take away from this, and that's that everything matters to some readers.

I haven't reviewed my author bio in some time. I don't even remember what it says, but I know it isn't optimized to hook the reader.

I can't stress this enough. Learn how to write an excellent description. Once you do, you'll be amazed at the percentage of books with horrible descriptions. Yes, even of the top 100 sellers on Amazon by authors who are household names, almost all have poorly written descriptions.

When you've come to understand the difference between effective descriptions and not, you'll have a competitive advantage over the other books that are trying to steal away your readers.

At this point, you may be wondering, *How do you figure out the conversion rate?*

That's a great question. I'll show you how to calculate that in an upcoming chapter. But first things first, my reader friend. We must first discuss how to analyze a platform before investing our smartly-earned capital.

5

WHERE SHOULD I INVEST MY ADVERTISING DOLLARS?

W here one should invest their advertising dollars is one of the most important questions an author/publisher can spend time thinking about. It isn't an easy question to answer, but there is an easy way to "do the math."

Don't worry, I'll tell you how to use a few cells in Excel to handle the math part.

The reason it isn't such an easy question is there are other questions to answer first.

"What is the goal of the advertising campaign?" is the first one.

But Brian, isn't that an easy question? To sell books and make money. You remember the game "systemless orphans, don't you?"

Of course, one of the goals of an advertising campaign is to sell books. But many factors determine whether an author is going to sell a book to the reader opening an ad. A couple of the basics are cover design and a clever description. Having reviews that help readers decide is important, too. So is name recognition.

I don't have any name recognition. If I did, I wouldn't need to worry about all this stupid data stuff.

Well, even if you're a *New York Times* bestselling author making $100,000 every single month, understanding the data and asking the right questions can help you get to $200,000 a month. You'd be able to help a lot more orphans and possibly donate a bit to your local guinea pig rescue center. Guinea pigs are adorable. I digress.

Still, maybe you'd like to be a *New York Times* or *USA Today* best seller. Would you like to make it onto "a list"?

No, Brian, I don't want to be a world-renowned best seller and have people sing my praises far and wide. Okay, maybe I do. A little.

Well, that's just one example of a different goal for an advertising campaign. Another is to gain exposure by pushing one's book up the Amazon ranking lists. The higher one is on the ranking list, the better the chance of getting additional sales from people who were not part of the advertising target group. We call those organic sales because they were generated by people's searches, and not by an advertisement. They are a bonus.

Some other reasons for advertising beyond just sales are, author name recognition, series recognition, title recognition, and general discoverability. Many people do not buy a book the first time they see it. The more times a book shows up, the greater the chance the reader will have already seen it before and feel more comfortable giving it a try.

The reason we need to understand our goals is that some venues may make sense for reaching one goal but not for another.

But let's look at the most common reason to run an ad: to sell books. We don't spend all that time crafting our masterpiece just to have it sit on a virtual shelf unread.

BookBub vs. "the Others", "Should I Advertise on _____," and ROI

If you've been in the book business for longer than fifteen minutes, you've heard of the book promotion site BookBub.

For those who have only been here for fourteen minutes, let me explain what "The Bub" is and why they're important.

BookBub is easily the most effective book marketing site available, short of having Amazon take up your cause.

They are the King Makers.

If you spend any time in forums, you'll read about BookBub, and the two most common themes will be that their ads are expensive and that it is impossible to get an ad accepted.

Let's look at the idea that it is impossible to get accepted by BookBub.

It is true that they reject eighty percent of ad submissions. Some they reject because the book in question has a dreadful cover or too few reviews (they like to see fifty reviews) or maybe because the BookBub gatekeeper reviewed the first few pages of the book, and it was so poorly written it made Ernest Hemingway look good. (Yes, that was a shot at E.H.)

The main reason they reject so many books, though, is that demand for the ad slots *greatly* exceeds the supply. BookBub will not compromise the quality of their ads by running dozens of books each day (in each category), because their subscribers want only the best of the best.

The subscribers trust BookBub, and when BookBub sends out the daily email, there is an excellent chance that readers will give the suggested book a try, even if they've never heard of the author.

When I first started submitting to BookBub, I was filled with unbridled optimism that they would surely accept my masterpiece, *Henry Wood Detective Agency*, because it was the *Best Book Ever*. (This is Honorée, and I can attest: The book is *so good!*)

My optimism was quickly bridled via a rejection email that had the stench of form letter all over it.

For a day, I was in denial. I couldn't believe they had said "no." This was followed by a morning of anger that could only be quelled with a liberal application of bacon to my tongue. Then I wrote back and asked them to reconsider, but they wouldn't budge. Depression settled in for the next sixteen hours until I finally accepted that I would need to try again.

These are the five stages of BookBub rejection.

I don't know why they rejected my book initially, but I now suspect it was the cover. My original cover (see below) was a black-and-white masterpiece that paid homage to an Italian art deco artist from the 1930s and subtly gave the nod to the old detective movies of the 1950s.

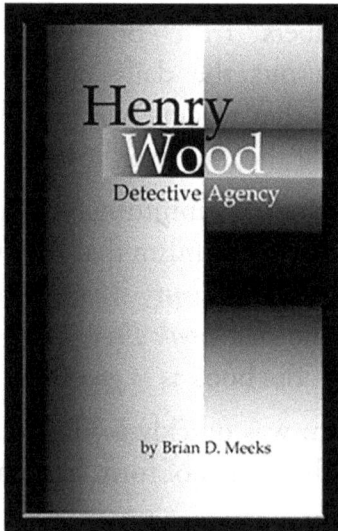

Apparently, the person who made the decision didn't have the Art History/Film Studies degree required to evaluate my art properly.

At the time, though, I didn't ask the question, "Does your cover suck?" because I was quite sure it didn't. I was wrong.

My first inclination was that BookBub might prefer books that were sold in more venues than just Amazon. I went wide and added the book to Barnes & Noble and Kobo.

Taking the bridle off my steed of optimism, I resubmitted after the "please don't bother us again for 30 days" period. They replied, "If you don't bridle that optimism you're going to hurt yourself. *No soup for you.*"

It was 2013, and I was hoping to get a 99-cent BookBub ad. Standing at 0-2 (zero wins, two losses for those whose arithmophobia extends even to sports statistics), I dusted myself off and decided to try submitting the second book in the series because it had a slightly more awesome cover, still with the nod to the Italian art deco dude.

Now I was at 0-3.

The ad, which I couldn't seem to get, cost $600. That's a lot of cabbage for someone who only had three books in their garden, but I had analyzed the price versus the expected outcome and had determined it was worth the gamble.

BookBub provides sales/download data for each genre on the pricing page. I don't remember exactly what the range was for the mystery genre, but I do remember that the average was around 2,200 sales, and since my book was the *Best Book Ever*, I reasoned that if I would get to the average number.

The math was easy. 2,200×0.35 (my revenue per book) = $770. If I spend $600 and get back $770 in sales, that's $170 in profit.

The ROI (Return on Investment, remember?) would be ($770 - $600)/ ($600) or 28.3%. And that would all happen in one day!

More than just the tiny pile of ducats, it would mean that over two thousand people who had never heard of Brian D. Meeks would be reading my book. That was worth a bunch, too.

Of course, I had two more books in the series at the time, and considering this one was the *Best Book Ever*, there would likely be some number of people who went on to buy books two and three at full price, $3.99 and $4.99 at the time.

And then there was the potential organic traffic. Getting over 2,000 sales in a single day would move my detective story into the top twenty on the overall Amazon ranking, per David Gaughran's book, *Let's Get Visible*.

It would also mean my book would rank among the top few books on the sub-genre lists and likely would reach number one.

Surely, with even a day atop those lists, the legions of mystery/detective fans who also appreciate a subtle Italian art deco artist reference cover, would start snapping up my books (and the sequels), launching me onto the cover of *Eligible Author Monthly* and leading to numerous offers of amour from the bibliophile *Sports Illustrated* swimsuit supermodel set.

This was my analysis, and it was only partially flawed. There were no supermodels.

The reality is that one does get a lot of exposure from a BookBub ad, and there are countless numbers of people who have made their way onto *The New York Times* best seller list with BookBub being the driving force behind their ascent.

The important thing was that I was thinking about more than just the $600. In almost every business decisions one makes, there are many more things to consider than just the immediate bottom line. What's the value of a *"New York Times* best seller" moniker? What's the value of a "#1 *New York Times* best seller"?

I don't know the value of either, but I'm reasonably confident that among any group of 1.5 million readers there will be some portion of them who are impressed by authors who have achieved that distinction.

Within that group, there are those who, at least at a subconscious level, ascribe more weight to an author who has reached number one.

Of course, this was all a moot point in my story because they kept taking the bridle off my horse.

I kept trying. After the eighth rejection, there was only one possibility left: The cover wasn't good enough.

I hired someone to create a new cover. It was much better than the one I designed. I then spent $250 to run a test ad, which I'll discuss in a later chapter. That test proved it was a vastly superior cover at getting people to give my book a chance.

This time when I submitted my book to BookBub, it got accepted. I galloped around my house with a joy usually reserved for children coming down the stairs at Christmas. The ad was a success. I was in the door and sure that all my future ad requests would be granted. BookBub loved me.

My next ad request was rejected.

As of the writing of this tome, I've had twelve BookBub ads accepted and probably close to twenty-six rejections. The point is, it did get easier, but rejections are still part of the process.

That's great, Brian, but I wasn't asking about BookBub.

True, but since BookBub is the most desirable, largest, and most expensive advertising venue, I use it as the benchmark by which I gauge their competitors.

In all my BookBub ads I've seen an ROI of no worse than 500% and usually much better.

Because they provide us with a breakdown of subscribers by genre, we're able to quickly calculate the value of their competitors by doing a comparison. Because the BookBub numbers are always changing, I'm going to create a fictitious genre for this example: GP.

Let's say you have a new book in the GP genre, but you've been turned down for a BookBub ad. In the GP genre on BookBub, there are 1,000,000 subscribers. At BookBub's current CPM ad rates, it would cost $260 to run a 99-cent ad, if you were to get one. On average, BookBub tells us that the GP genre generates 940 sales. You know that you make 35 cents for each book sold at price.

$940 \times 0.35 = \$329$, less the $260 to run the ad, gives you a profit of $69.

But you haven't gotten a BookBub ad. You believe you could get an XYZBooks ad. Their ad only costs $20 and goes out to 40,000 subscribers. Is that a good deal?

Well, let's see how much that ad would cost if we paid that rate to reach BookBub's subscribers.

The first thing to consider is that with very few exceptions, most advertising venues don't break out the readers by the genre they prefer, so 40,000 readers does not mean 40,000 GP readers. Some of those readers only read romance, others like detective stories, others want Christian-themed books, and a portion of them want to read about guinea pigs.

But since we don't know the breakout, and we're going to give the venue the benefit of the doubt, we're going to assume that all 40,000 readers are interested in *every* genre possible. (A ridiculous assumption, to be sure, but you'll soon see why that doesn't matter.)

Okay, so if we assume all 40,000 readers like GP, and we divide 40,000 into one million, we are left with the BookBub pool of readers being twenty-five times larger than the XYZBooks pool.

So, if we take the cost of the XYZBooks ad times twenty-five, we get an apples-to-apples (sort of) comparison. The cost of the ad from XYZ Books would be $500 using their ad rates to reach a BookBub-sized reader pool. That's $240 more expensive than BookBub charges. Wow!

But, if one is making 500% ROI at the BookBub prices, then even at the XYZBooks prices the ad should still be profitable, right?

Well, yes, if all 40,000 XYZBooks readers were fans of the GP genre. They're not. It's only a fraction, probably a tiny fraction. If our ad were for a Romance or Mystery book (the two most highly read genres) I'd cut that number in half. For other genres, it might be one-third or less.

Let's redo the math with 10,000 readers.

10,000 divided into 1 million is 100. 100 x $20 equals $2,000 for an ad at this price to reach a Bookbub-sized audience. Your chances of having a positive ROI on this ad are slim. And that's not even taking into account the possibility that readers in the XYZBooks pool may be less likely to purchase a book than BookBub's readers, which would lower the ROI even more.

So, what would be a fair price for their ad?

That's an excellent question. I could go through the math, but I wouldn't pay more than $3.

It is interesting to note that when BookBub was a young company with a much smaller mailing list, they charged authors zero.

XYZbooks.com wants to make money—I get that—and $20 doesn't seem like much to ask, but if my goal is to make money on the ad, then I'd have to pass.

Does that mean that I would never advertise with them? Nope, it doesn't mean that at all. In fact, I probably would, but only under special circumstances.

6

USING DATA TO MAKE CRITICAL DECISIONS

Understanding your numbers can help you decide whether to enroll in an exclusive program like KDP Select, or whether (as a freelance writer) to write for just one magazine, or even when it's time to go full-time as a writer! Let's look at each one of these in detail.

Brian's got your formulas and Honorée will weigh in with some perspective.

WHAT IS THE VALUE OF KDP SELECT PAGE READS?

As of the writing of this chapter (note: it changes monthly), each page read by a Kindle Unlimited subscriber nets the author/publisher $0.00537, or just over one-half of one cent. It doesn't seem like a lot, but a KU page isn't exactly like one page of written text. It's smaller.

Because each Kindle user can choose the size of their font, and because Kindle devices vary wildly in screen size, Amazon has created normalized page counts. This number can be found for each book about forty-eight hours after the book is enrolled in KDP Select.

On the Bookshelf, to the far right of your book(s) is an ellipsis (...). Click on the ellipsis and a drop-down box appears. Choose the third option on the list, "KDP Select Info." The next page has all the information about your book, its enrollment period, and in the section titled "Earn Royalties from the KDP Select Global Fund," at the bottom, your Kindle Edition Normalized Page Count (KENPC: Kindle Edition Normalized Page Count) v1.0. For my book, *Secret Doors: The Challenge*, the number is 282. The print version of the book is right at 200, so you can see the number tends to be higher than one might expect.

This means that for that book, if someone reads it in its entirety, the author/publisher will receive $282 \times 0.00537 = \$1.51$. I have this book priced at $4.99, so this is less than the $3.45 I would make from a sale.

The question is, would the person who gave the book a try as part of their KU subscription have bought the book otherwise? We don't know the answer to that, but I suspect there is a portion of KU subscribers who only read books that are part of their subscription. For them, the answer would be "no."

To the person who jumps to the conclusion that $1.51 is a bad deal for the author, I'd have to respectfully disagree. Having a book enrolled in KDP Select offers advantages beyond just the revenue, especially to the newer author who doesn't have a fan base yet.

The obvious reason is exposure because the KU subscriber may be willing to try a book by an author they've never heard of because it's free to them. But there's more to it than that.

The reason Honorée and I love KDP Select is because the page reads metric offers a glimpse into the effectiveness of changes made to a book's cover, description, or if one is running ads, the ad copy itself.

Imagine you're a new author who has a book that sells ten copies per month. That means most days there aren't any sales. Let's say you are tweeting, writing blog posts, and using social media to get people to check out your book, but you're disappointed by the results.

You may be driving people to your Amazon detail page, but not enough of them are hitting the purchase button.

What's the problem? Does the cover suck? Is the description not inviting?

The easiest thing to change is the description, but with such low volume sales it may be impossible to tell if the change is helping to improve conversions.

A Touch to Die For is a thriller and had been out for two years when I decided to spend a little time driving traffic to its page. The book was only selling one to three copies per month, and I was getting a few thousand page reads per month. That's equivalent to another three sales.

My gut told me that the description was crap, so I changed it. The next day my page reads jumped. I didn't have any sales, but a few more people had chosen to give the book a try. This is not significant data, and one day does not a best seller make, so I didn't do any dancing or anything.

Without changing any of my advertising or social media efforts, the page reads continued to average about 35% per day more than before I had changed the description. This increase remained for weeks. I decided to do the test again on my satire, which was easily my best seller, averaging eight to ten sales per day and about 2,500 page reads per month.

The description was reworked, and the next day I saw an immediate jump in page reads, just like with the thriller.

Here's the thing, I wasn't making a dramatic change to the descriptions, either. In both cases, I simply put three quotes from readers at the top after a header "Praise for...:"

That's it.

That single change had convinced KU subscribers to give my books a try at a greater rate than before, and the increase didn't fade. Both books still have a greater number of page reads per day than they did before the change.

The satire, because it sells more than the thriller, also showed an increase in sales, which I think I can attribute to the description change. But I can't prove it. Even at ten sales per day, the numbers are still too small to draw definitive conclusions from, but I can say that overall revenue (page reads and sales) for both books is up nicely.

Making the decision to be exclusive to Amazon KDP Select has not only allowed me to increase my revenue it has also provided me with data that let me better understand my business. The latter point may be the most valuable of all when one considers the life of a catalog of books.

Does this mean one shouldn't go wide and distribute through Apple iBooks, Barnes & Noble, Kobo, etcetera? No, not at all. Like all aspects of the book business, this decision must be made based upon the current state of one's business. The question *Should I go wide?* may have to be asked every three or four months for many years because today's answer may not be the same as tomorrow's.

Honorée here. You must think about your writing as a business. This thinking perspective is actually as important to your author business as your writing. Every business person has a plan and goals and regularly evaluates both. While there are dissenting opinions about enrolling one's books in KDP Select, we believe the best decision you can make is the one you've carefully thought through. Also, you will probably receive advice from multiple sources. Something to keep in mind when listening to someone's advice is to use their own data as a guide about whether or not to accept their advice. For example, someone who has written a few books must have books that sell and rank highly in their categories on Amazon for more than a few weeks or months, and they must have a high Amazon author rank for me to give weight to their advice. I do believe everyone has the best intentions when telling you to launch your book for free, or to "just use any cover," but if they haven't created the author business you aspire to have, think twice before taking their advice. Okay? Okay. Back to Brian.

How Do I Decide What Freelance Work to Accept?

Freelance work is an interesting subject. It can be an incredible source of income that gets one over the hump and into the life of a full-time writer.

Before my books started doing well, I considered going this route but could never pull the trigger. For me, it just didn't make sense because I couldn't get past the idea of writing 10,000 words and then only getting paid for it once.

All the content I was writing would eventually become novels that would earn me royalties for the rest of my life—I plan to live to 350—and getting paid one time for my creativity just wasn't something I felt could do.

Does that mean that you should turn down freelance work? No, it does not. There may be dozens (or hundreds) of projects that you could bang out with little thought because the subject is in an area in which you have some expertise. There are other advantages, too. If the freelance work is going to get you exposure because you get a "byline," then the thoughtful article on "making talking guinea pig movies" might lead to more sales of your book, *Piggywood: The Lucrative World of Guinea Pig Cinema.*

There is also the confidence one gets from writing for others and having it accepted. You may well find you have another level of skill when you're not worried about the piece being good enough for submission.

Though I never went the freelance route, I do think it's a great way to gain experience, confidence, exposure (in some cases), and earn some money. I would *not*, however, suggest you ghostwrite entire novels (or books) for someone else who intends to slap their name on them and profit for the rest of their life. In that case, just publish it yourself.

Honorée again. Brian gives such great advice, and I agree completely with him. There are two other considerations you might want to keep in mind: the number of eyes on your words (a.k.a. "discoverability"), and of course, how easily you crank out the words.

If you can write a freelance piece in a short time and still stick to your regular production schedule (which is based on your tightly-designed plan, right?), *and* said piece increases your discoverability, then I say *Go for it!* The more you write, the more you'll be able to write.

Recently, I had a major platform ask me to write a series of blogs for them in 2017. I have almost a dozen books on my production schedule for the year, and I had to consider whether I had the time and ability to say, "Yes!" (Which I did.) I believe the exposure and additional income is worth the time, energy, and capacity it will take.

When evaluating work, money should not be your only consideration. Evaluate every request with the same set of criteria you would use if you were already fully committed and were making more than enough money. Evaluate opportunities from the position of strength. *Do I truly want to do this? Is it for my highest and best good? Would it still make sense to say yes, if I were already earning a living from my writing?* This is the best place from which to decide. Another thing to consider is how effortlessly you're able to write. If it takes every ounce of your being to work on your long-term creative efforts, and taking on an additional project will drain your creative well, it might not be the best idea. However, if you can complete an additional project without too much of a sacrifice, it might make sense.

Which leads us to the million-dollar question:

When Can I Go Full-Time?

Brian here. I made the decision to leave my part-time job after I had a moment of clarity. Things were going well. I was making about eight times as much selling books as what I made from my job, but I kept going to work two days per week. Part of the reason was that I was using my income from the job to cover my expenses. That left all the revenue from my book sales to be used for more editing, cover art, and advertising.

One day, though, I realized the part-time job was folly, even though I did enjoy it. I had been working on a half-dozen writing projects and had even hired someone to help. As I was working on that "aha" day, I realized I was paying someone $13.50 an hour to work on a project I couldn't work on because I was at my part-time job making ten dollars an hour. I put in my notice that day.

It was the best decision of my life.

I could have probably left the job a couple of months earlier, but I don't have any regrets. I left when it was 100% clear that I was making the right decision. I never wanted to be in a situation where I was stressed out about being a full-time author because I knew that would impair my ability to write. I hate writing when I'm stressed, and I often go into a napping frenzy that could be compared to hibernation, which is not at all productive.

I would wager that you'll know when it feels right. Trust your gut.

Honorée here. I wrote about having a prosperity mindset in *Prosperity for Writers*. I agree with Brian wholeheartedly and think it's important to go full time when the timing feels right. I suggest an income target of 150% of what you need to live. In other words, if you need $5,000 a month to live on, your income target becomes $7,500. From a pure numbers perspective, I suggest you make the leap when you have enough financial reserve that you can weather just about any storm that comes your way. For me, it was having three months' worth of reserve at my suggested 150% target, in this scenario $22,500. I had enough reserve to pay all expected and unexpected expenses for three months (closer to four and a half months without anything unexpected coming up) even if I made no income. Assuming you're already making some income, and perhaps are close to your goal, you won't need to tap into your reserve much (if at all) after you've left your job.

If, on the other hand, your risk tolerance is high, and you're comfortable with "leap and the net will appear," then go for it. I've done that more than a few times in my life and everything turned out, thankfully, just fine.

7

USING THE NUMBERS TO MAKE MORE MONEY

B rian here.

You judgmental bastard, I thought as I saw the middle-aged hipster pick up a book, look at the cover, and then set it down with a contempt usually reserved for domestic wine. It horrified me to think he had just done the unthinkable: He had judged the book by its cover…and found it wanting.

The thing about old axioms is that they survive because of the grain of truth for which they are *axiomated* (I know that's not a word, but it should be).

TEST COVERS

So you think your cover is good enough? (Hint: it probably isn't if your book isn't selling well.)

Many Indie authors have struggled with figuring out a cover for their masterpiece and often err on the side of affordable. This is a mistake made repeatedly. I know, I've made it.

As I mentioned earlier, for my first book, *Henry Wood Detective Agency*, I had decided I was handy enough with Photoshop to do it myself. I based my design on the art deco work of a little-known Italian designer from the 1930s that I loved. My book, which takes place in 1955, slightly after the art deco period but still within shouting distance, has a *noir* feel, and I believed it would lend itself well to that style.

For hours, I tried different designs until I hit upon the one that I was sure would take the world by storm. I went with my cover, and it was nothing but sunny skies from the reader, and not a sign of inclement weather on the horizon.

Six months later I had had a few negative comments about the cover from people who don't have degrees in Art History and couldn't appreciate my clever reference (including, apparently, the BookBub gatekeeper from Chapter Five). Clearly, something needed to be done, so I hired a professional knowledgable in the ways of art deco. I spent $350 on the new cover.

Here is where keeping data taught me a valuable lesson. Because I track every promotion I run, I looked back at the first Free Day I had run when the book had my cover and then created an almost duplicate promotion for the book with the new cover. They were both done with the same advertising venue, on the same day of the week, and I refrained from changing anything beyond that to make sure my data was as clean as possible.

A clever data person will point out that because I used the same venue for the second promotion, a portion of those subscribers already had my book, so that would skew the numbers in favor of the original cover. I knew this but still wanted to see what would happen.

At 10:01 p.m. on both days I reviewed how many free downloads the book had and the difference in results was telling. April 2013 had 1,161 downloads, and October had 2,589. It should be noted that the venue I advertised with hadn't grown their list much between the two promotions, though it might have grown a little.

The point is that with more than twice as many downloads, the new professionally made cover outperformed the original by 123%.

That is a big number, and one needs to understand that impact it has on one's sales (or free downloads) every single day. A new author is known to nobody, and the cover is the best chance of getting the avid reader who enjoys discovering new writers to give it a try. This is how one gets their writing career going.

It's also why one should keep all their data because, when a change is made, testing the new version and seeing positive or negative results can help with future decisions. Now, I hire a professional for all my covers. It makes a big difference.

Still, it can be difficult to pull the trigger on spending so much money on something we don't know will ever sell. Here's the deal, if you have a bad cover on a great book, you'll never know if you could have achieved your dream because nobody will give it a try. If you have a great cover on a crappy book, you'll probably fail in the long run because the writing sucks, but you'll still have some sales and likely get your money back. Even if you don't, the peace of mind of knowing you gave your novel every chance to succeed will be worth the price of a good cover.

If you're still not convinced, or if you think you'll use the crappy cover until you have enough money for the good one, try looking at it another way. Spending $300 to $400 on a quality cover is probably less than you spent on that high-end golf club or those shoes you just had to have for the wedding. And neither of them will have a shot at producing an income stream (unless you're a scratch golfer or a hooker), so why not divert some of your monthly Starbucks budget to your dream? It will be worth it.

(See picture below)

Original　　New

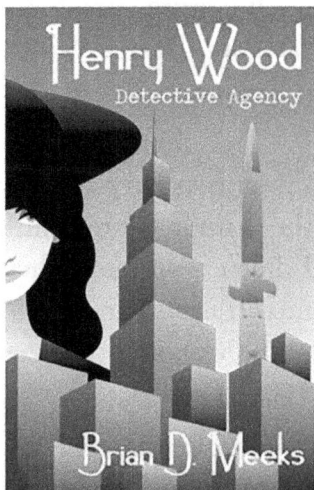

Who will win?

Now you've got a Book Bub ad. What should you do with it?

I'm sitting in the Hamburg Inn No. 2 in Iowa City today, eating a Denver omelet and writing. It's January 4, 2016, and a few hours ago, I got accepted for my thirteenth BookBub ad and only my second one at 99 cents. It's a perfect time to talk about what to do after the excitement subsides from reading the acceptance email.

First, read the email carefully. One does not always get accepted for the advertisement they requested. This was the case today. I submitted my book, *Underwood, Scotch, and Wry* in the Literature genre, not because it's literature, but because they didn't have a satire category. It's the genre this book has been accepted to before.

The literature genre has over one million subscribers. My book was accepted for an advert in the humor genre. Humor is a much better fit, and I didn't even know they had added that genre to the mix. It is new and has a much smaller subscriber base (250,000), and the average number of sales per ad is 500.

This is valuable information to consider, and if I hadn't read the email carefully, I might not have known the book was in the smaller category. I'll be approaching the promotion differently than I would have otherwise.

After reading the acceptance and understanding when my ad would run (January 17), I immediately went in and set up a Kindle Countdown Deal starting at 1:00 a.m. on the 17th and running through 1:00 a.m. on the 19th. (Note: a Kindle Countdown Deal is one of the benefits of being exclusive with Amazon. It allows the author to change the price to below $2.99 and still get the 70% royalty during the promotion of up to seven days.)

That's all I'm going to do for this promotion besides gather data on the day of the email blast.

What if it were an acceptance in a larger genre? Would that change my plans?

I write a mystery series, and that genre has over 3 million readers who receive the daily emails. This category affords one an opportunity to try to go for a list (*New York Times* or *USA Today*).

It should be noted that the *New York Times* ebook lists require that the book receives reported sales on more than one venue. This makes their list unreachable for those who choose to be exclusive to Amazon. If one wants to be a *New York Times* bestselling author, then going wide is the only option.

Let's look at how one might approach a 99-cent (or $1.99 or $2.99) promotion if they've got their books on more than one platform, and the goal is to sell enough units to crack the list. This number can be 10,000 for fiction or 15,000 for non-fiction in a single week (Sunday through Saturday for the NY Times). The number of sales required varies from week to week, and certain times of the year require much higher numbers, but we're going to use the 10K number for our exercise.

Ten thousand sales are a bunch. That's 1,429 per day. Hitting that number on the day of the BookBub ad won't be a problem if one is in one of the major genres, but what about the other days? And how does this impact our strategy?

First, the day of the week that your advert will run has a significant impact on the chances. One might think the best day would be Sunday because the book gets a big boost in rankings on the first day of the week and then has six more days to try to hit the number needed for the list.

I would argue that the optimal day would be Monday or better yet, Tuesday.

When submitting your book for a BookBub ad, one can request a specific date or choose the "flexible" option. If the goal is to make a list, then trying to get a particular date may be the best move, though it may also make it more challenging to get the ad.

So, why is Monday or Tuesday better than Sunday?

Having a day before the BookBub ad comes out allows one to try to get additional ads at other venues the day before the BookBub email blast hits. This can be incredibly helpful when one considers the value of the organic exposure from being ranked near the top of the Amazon Top 100 list.

I've studied the results of many Free Day promotions, all of which my book made it to the top three overall, and the organic free downloads unrelated to the BookBub blast make up between 20% and 25% of the total. The exposure is important.

It's equally important, if not more so, for the Top 100 paid list. There are literally hundreds of thousands of people (if not millions) who may be exposed to your book because it's ranked #7 overall who have never heard of you. And with a BookBub ad in the right category, selling the 3,000 to 5,000 copies needed to land on the first page of that list (books one through twenty) is very possible.

Every hour on that first page is gold. The best hours are in the evening after people get home from work. Again, from my data on other promotions I've seen a spike in sales (or free downloads) from the hours of 6 to 10 p.m.

So, we want to ensure our book is ranked as highly as possible as quickly as possible. The thing about BookBub ads is once the blast goes out, and the sales start pouring in, the Amazon ranking doesn't change right away. It can take hours for the next update to hit, and that first jump won't be representative of where your book should be at all. It might have jumped to #708 overall, but that's not as helpful as the next update when it's #57, and the one after that where your precious baby is #5.

This brings me to my point about putting out some ads on other venues the day before your BookBub ad. It's like priming the pump to get the machine running. Right now, your book is ranked 65,287th. Three ads with other venues that bring in a couple of hundred sales should get it ranked in the top 1,000.

This means that after the BookBub email blast goes out your book is already doing well (which may also help sway a few additional buyers to give it a try). But it also means that the first ranking update may be enough to get you in the top 100 by three o'clock, and the next one may land you on that first page just as people are getting home from work. Those extra sales from the ads the day before give one an excellent chance to maximize the effectiveness of a BookBub ad.

It should be noted that this isn't enough, usually, to land oneself a coveted spot on *The New York Times* best seller list, but it's a move in the right direction. The next step is to fill up the days after the ad with as many promotions at other venues as one can land. This is the one case where I don't care about the ROI of an ad and how good a value the price is because the goal is to make a list, and every sale counts.

Given a choice with the other venues, I'd try to schedule as many promotions as I could for the day after the BookBub ad and then fill in the other days with the ones that could give me the date I wanted.

This is also a very good time to plan for a social media scheduled blast.

I hate scheduling tweets. It feels disingenuous to me, but in this case, I'd plan a bunch of pithy tweets to go out once an hour for the entire week. I'd also try to spend a fair amount of time on Twitter during that week. My Twitter focus wouldn't be on promoting the book but just on interacting with people about whatever tickles my fancy. It's good to have non-promotional tweets in one's timeline to make the promotional ones not looks so spammy.

Spending a little energy on Facebook and Google+ can also help. And remember your mailing list. You'll want to explain what you're trying to accomplish in the newsletter because some of your most ardent fans may buy a copy or give one to their friend just to support you.

The one other reason it might be better to be on a Monday or Tuesday is that the *USA Today* list runs from Monday to Sunday. There are worse things in the world than aiming for the *New York Times* list and landing on the *USA Today* list.

It should be noted I've *not* made a list...yet. So, I might be full of crap, but I don't think I am. This business is all about math and data. The bottom line is: the more books one sells in a week, the better the chance of making a list.

This strategy will help you achieve that goal if it's something you'd like to do.

As for my recent BookBub acceptance, it isn't a large enough group of readers to give me a reasonable chance at a list, so I'm focused on maximizing revenue. Therefore, I've chosen the Countdown deal. When one is a member of KDP Select, the Countdown deal is one of the benefits, and when one is running such a deal the author still gets 70% even if the price has been set lower than $2.99 (the point at which the royalty drops to 35%).

There is one more thing to consider, and that's how long to run the promotional price.

When one gets moved up the charts to the rarified air that is the first page on the Top 100 overall, it means a lot of exposure to people who don't know you or at what the book is typically priced. So, it begs the question when should I put the price back up to full again?

If I were going for one of the lists, I'd leave the book at 99 cents for the whole week. All I want are units sold; I don't care about profits.

Since I'm not going for a list with the current ad, I'll be putting the price back to full one day after the BookBub ad. I'd expect maybe 500 sales during the promotion which won't get me to the Top 100, but it will move the book up the rankings of the sub-lists, and that means, to a lesser extent, organic eyeballs.

Those organic readers won't know that the book got to the #1 spot in that category by being 99 cents. All they'll see is a book that looks good at a reasonable price, in my case $4.99.

After earning seventy cents per sale for a couple of days, a few sales that garner $3.45 (factoring in the delivery cost) will be a welcome addition to the bottom line.

Using the Numbers When You're Planning a Series

This section may offend your artistic sensibilities, so be warned. If one wants to find the most efficient path to the day they quit their day job to become a full-time author, then these considerations are part of that equation.

I'm talking about the length of a book. You're planning an epic fantasy series involving wizards, elves, warriors, and battling guinea pigs wielding the screech of death. It will span generations, and millions will die (though not the guinea pigs, because that would be wrong).

Those who read epic series know that each book runs for many hundreds of pages sometimes bordering on a gazillion. That's what you, as an avid reader, have grown to expect, and so that's what you plan to write. The first book will be 154,000 words!

No.

This is a bad strategy from the get-go for many reasons.

1. It takes three times as long to write 150,000 words as it does 50,000.

2. Nobody knows who you are so you'll probably only to be able to charge $4.99 regardless.

3. If you write one book instead of three smaller books as part of a trilogy, you're hampering your ability to do some great marketing things.

Warning: This is *not* to say you should take an existing book and simply chop it into thirds. That is almost always a horrible idea.

What I'm suggesting is that you plan your story to have three great stories with satisfying endings that leave a thread or two unresolved to take the reader into the next story.

Again, I know you're cringing at the idea of writing only 50,000 words. It makes you feel cheap, a sellout, the dregs of writing society, but in an age of short attention spans, people won't notice if they have the next book to jump into.

I did this in 2015 with my post-apocalyptic space opera, *The Magellan Apocalypse*. Inspiration hit me like a ton of muses one day in January. Ideas just kept pouring forth, and I couldn't stop them. I wrote the first book in two weeks. It came in at 50,000 words.

I made the decision to write the next one right away while the first one was being edited. The second book took six weeks because I had fewer ideas, and so it was more of a challenge. It was finished about the time the book one, *Map Runners*, was back from my second editor.

At that point, I made the decision that I'm not recommending as a strategy, but it worked for me. The third book would be written, and then I'd release all three in one month. Again, I'm not saying one should wait, but for me, I was curious if it would help with the launch. I'm convinced it did, but I'm also sure that some people might use that strategy as an excuse to procrastinate. Don't do that.

The point is that by launching the three books on Sept 1st, 8th, and 22nd, I got to see data about the read-through. For this series, I see about 70% read through from book one to two, and about 90% of those who go to book two, also pick up book three.

Now, going back to thinking about my 150,000 words. I could have released it as one book, and there wouldn't have been any read-through. You know what else there wouldn't have been? A boxed set of all three books.

Yes, not only do you get three books, but you get a fourth product to sell. I released the boxed set in late October, and it has done very well. Its price point is $8.99. I would have never been able to charge that for the same book if it was just one book because nobody knows me, but as a collection of three books priced individually at $4.99, $8.99 is a bargain.

Some of you may be wondering about cannibalization of sales by offering a boxed set, and I'll get to that in a subsequent chapter.

Using the Numbers Even After You Think Your Book or Your Series is Done

If you recall, I showed you people *do* judge a book by its cover. This isn't hard to believe, as we've all been bombarded by advertising images our whole lives. I know from personal experience that product placement in sitcoms works, because *every* time I see someone eating Chinese food, I must have some.

I believe I convinced you that a high-quality cover matters. What if I told you that I have just hired a new cover artist to replace the professional *Henry Wood* cover that did so well in the previous example? Well, I have.

The reason is that though I saw an improvement from the first professional cover, I did *not* conclude that I had reached perfection. This new cover upgrade cost $750, and I'll be spending that same amount, or more, on each of the four Henry Wood books. I believe based on the numbers that it will attract more eyeballs than the current one, and that over the long term (you remember I intend to live to 350), I'll easily recoup the cost.

The point is that I recognized an opportunity because I didn't assume the cover was optimized.

Using the numbers to keep yourself on track to achieve goals, such as writing 1,000 words a day for a year equals 365,000 words or the equivalent of six 60,000 word novels!

Author Goal-Setting

Setting goals and tracking results can greatly improve one's productivity. As you know by now, I love numbers. I also like making goals. The truth of the matter is that sticking with a plan of so many words per day is something I've struggled with historically, but I keep getting better.

Don't ever assume that because I'm a full-time author I'm a well-oiled machine. I set goals, reach some of them, fail on others, and am continually trying to improve. It is a constant struggle, but I do see improvement anytime I look back six months to how I was before.

I've written a novel in five hours short of a fortnight (two weeks). It's 50,000 words, does well, and was a fine example of setting up a plan and sticking to it. The second book in the series took six weeks. It was the same length, but I didn't stick to my plan. The third book took around ten weeks. I played a lot of video games during that time.

The thing about habits is that when one falls out of following them, it can be discouraging. However, I've found that each time I revisit the habit, staying with it gets easier, and I stick with it longer. So, if at first you don't stick with it, try and try again.

We've covered some complex ideas and strategies around numbers. And if you're overwhelmed, Honorée can relate. There is a very simple, yet important, aspect of numbers you can start using instantly. It's a very basic strategy: one you probably already know, and may even have used from time to time. The strategy is simply set a goal to write 1,000 new words per day, every single day. Every single day may mean every single weekday, or if you're an overachiever, you may write on weekends and holidays, too. If you write 1,000 words every day of the year, you'll write 365,000 words, which is the equivalent of approximately ten decent sized nonfiction books, or six full-length novels.

If you're following the model of write, publish, repeat, as we do, you'll appreciate that you don't need to write for hours and hours at a time, racking up thousands or tens of thousands of words during any given writing session. When you master the skill of writing faster, you'll be cranking out book after book after book, and getting it all done pretty much before 9 AM. Which leaves you the rest of the day to conquer global domination, or something a little simpler like learning a second language.

Honorée has a simple spreadsheet where every day she tracks the amount of time she writes (usually about an hour, but sometimes only 15 minutes) and the number of words she writes (usually around thousand, sometimes only 500, other days she'll have a word gust of up to 5,000). On another page of the spreadsheet, she tracks the money side of her book business. You can design a spreadsheet that fits your needs, but of course we've provided one for you, and you'll find it here HonoreeCorder.com/m3bonuses.

There are several remarkable things about keeping a spreadsheet. One of them is you'll be able to see your progress. Seeing a child you haven't seen for a long time, it appears as though they've grown almost overnight. By tracking your word count and your income, you'll be able to see and track your incremental growth over time. There are few things as cool as being able to look back and see how far you've come and how quickly you got there in the overall scheme of life. It's especially cool when you got there by doing just a little bit every single day.

8

CALCULATING YOUR COPY'S CONVERSION

Knowing how well our book descriptions converts visitors into purchasers is important. The reason I give a range for my descriptions is that we don't have exact numbers. We need to make some assumptions to get a reasonable approximation of the number. I love precision, but if I can't get perfect data, then I'll settle for reasonable data.

For this section, I think it's best just to jump into some numbers to demonstrate how I would calculate my conversion rate.

For my satire, *Underwood, Scotch, and Wry*, I run ads. Each day I know how many people click through to the book's Amazon page. This seems like an exact number, but it doesn't factor in the organic traffic of people finding the book on their own. There isn't anything I can do about that, so I use the click through number.

I spend a bunch on advertisements each day. Periodically, I'll shut off all my ads for a few days; this gives me a baseline of people that are finding my books organically through search or from having read one of my other books. I have a rough idea of the organic, but for this example, we're going to ignore that piece of the puzzle. I can tell you, though, that the vast majority of the people who visit my book's page are brought there from my ads.

Let's say there are 200 clicks on a given day and we assume they are all from a new ad. To figure out my conversion rate I need to know the number of book sales. Let's say it is ten sales. How many ad clicks does it take to get me one sale? I just divide the number of clicks by the number of sales: 200/10 = 20. So, I get one sale for every 20 clicks. That's a conversion rate of 1:20 or 5%.

But Brian, you said you were doing much better than that?

You've been paying attention. Two points.

Yes, I did, and I am.

Ten sales is not all of the conversions. Remember those KDP Select page reads we talked about before? There are more "sales," and they are downloads by people who are in Kindle Unlimited.

I don't know what percentage of the 200 people who clicked on my ad are KU subscribers, and I don't need to know. It suffices to say that some of them subscribe, and that's enough.

Because I'm not counting organic clicks by people who have searched for a term like Humor and Satire, the ad click-through number is lower than the number of people who actually view the Amazon page. This skews our data to look better than it really is, but that's fine because there is a bit of skewing going on in the number of sales, too.

This is important. The KU readers are real. Their conversions count. They generate real revenue via the KDP Select paid per page system.

Unfortunately, we don't know how many Kindle Unlimited subscribers downloaded *Underwood, Scotch, and Wry* in our example. If we did, we would simply add that number to the ten sales and recalculate.

What we do know is how many page reads we had that day.

Remember when I said "moving averages" were sometimes helpful? This is one of those times. I take the average number of KDP Select page reads over the previous seven days (before the new 200 click ad started running). This gives me a baseline.

Let's say I've been averaging 1,100 page reads on *Underwood, Scotch, and Wry* per day, but with the new ad that number jumps to 3,500. Those 2,400 additional page reads can be attributed to more people starting my novel because they converted.

To figure out how many people it took to get the 2,400 I make a conservative assumption that the people who downloaded the book read 100% of the way through in one day.

That, however, is not what happened. There may be some voracious readers who did just that but not all of them. Some people read only 50 pages, others 100, and one guy with terrible taste read only one page and gave up. I hate that guy.

Still, I need to start somewhere, so if I assume they read the entire book, I divide the 2,400 page reads by the number of pages for the Kindle version (KENPC), which is 300, and I know that at least eight people downloaded my book.

If we divide 200 by 18 (10 sales + 8 KU subscribers), our conversion is 1 in 11.1.

This is why I say the under-reporting of the numerator (200) is offset by the conservative estimate of the KU readers. A more likely scenario is that there were probably 16 people who downloaded the book, which would yield a 1 in 7.69 conversion.

Regardless of the assumptions we make, it is clear that my conversion is vastly better now than it was between 1 in 20 and 1 in 30.

We want precision when possible, but estimates to yield a reasonable understanding of what is going on are still miles better than never doing the math.

What is your conversion?

I can hear you sighing. Is the problem that your conversion rate is fine, but you don't know how to drive people to your book page?

That's a common problem. Let's talk about advertising a little more.

9

ADVERTISING TAKES WORK AND THE PATIENCE OF JOB

(BUT YOU'VE GOT THIS, WE PROMISE!)

A dvertising is hard.

It takes a lot of time, money, and patience.

Brian here. As I've mentioned, I use lots of different venues. The most popular is using Facebook ads. This is an incredibly challenging place to advertise and is beyond the scope of this book.

Still, I recommend adding Facebook advertising as a course of study to your list. You may not be ready yet, and that's fine. One can drive traffic using Twitter, posting on Facebook for free, or any of the other social media platforms. I drive some traffic using Pinterest and rarely spend more than $1 per day.

Pinterest is one venue that I intend to investigate further because I believe it could be a reasonably profitable move with a lot of study and work.

Regardless, you should be thinking about trying to find ways to drive people to your page. The benefits are more than just the sales directly attributed to your efforts. Each sale you drive to your book's page helps your book's ranking and is a conversion. We don't know exactly how Amazon factors in conversion to their page ranks, but we can be sure they do.

Better conversion and rankings help your book get discovered by people outside of your sphere of influence (Twitter, Pinterest, Facebook, Google+, friends and family).

The question becomes, how do you know the number of people who click on a link?

There are several ways to track responders:

- Use a link shortener like Bit.ly
- Use an affiliate link
- Send people to a landing page on your website then have a link you can track that goes to Amazon

I try to use more than one because one can't always assume the numbers are 100% accurate. Having multiple data points can help one home in on the truth. All of this requires work. I'm not going to sugar coat it. The suggestions I've made have required many hours of time away from writing.

This may not be what you want to hear. I'm sorry. Don't quit on me. If you can get through the next few excruciatingly painful paragraphs, there is some good news. Yes, that was another open loop.

But the cold hard facts are that my monthly sales are over $10,000 per month because I devote nearly all of my time (95%) to the areas discussed in the book. Only 5% of my time is writing.

That may be a punch in the gut. Understand this: the massive amount of time I'm spending is like building a solid foundation for my writing/publishing house. Each of these pieces, once built, serves me for years to come.

I don't need to learn how to write good ad copy every year. Learning how to track my data only happens once. Gaining an understanding of how to spend advertising dollars profitably is front-loaded, meaning that though I'll need to keep current, it won't take as much time as it did to learn initially.

Furthermore, many of these tasks can be given to an assistant, whom you'll be able to pay from the sizable revenue you've generated by devoting time to your business.

There is one other secret. Once you start using data to find ways to make your beloved book earn money for you, it won't seem like a chore. It's fun.

Now for the good news.

I don't know what you thought about my sales. I certainly know people who make much more than $10,000 every month, but I also know a lot of authors who would be thrilled with that number.

It isn't the number that's important; it's that I've gotten to that point by doing all the things mentioned. Poorly.

It's true. I'm a hot mess.

I've succeeded thus far despite doing a crappy job of implementing my great ideas. You remember a few pages back when I was talking about how I improved my conversion on the book descriptions?

It's a couple of hours work for a lifetime of increased sales. Did I do it for all twelve of my novels and my two boxed sets to maximize my revenue?

No.

I rewrote four of my descriptions, got to *A Touch to Die For*, my first thriller got stuck, and stopped. I could have jumped to the boxed set, or the other books in the Magellan series, which would have been easy. Instead, I bought a new 40-inch ultra-high-definition TV and a new Xbox. This led to a three-day Halo binge.

Before I could get back to the descriptions, I got distracted by another bright and shiny data idea.

That's how it is with me. I figure something out, and it's profitable but don't do a good job of implementation. Nobody sucks at this as much as I do. You certainly don't.

But wait…there's more.

For about three years, readers have politely written me asking when the paper versions of my books would be out. My answer was always, "Soon."

The voice in my head was disgusted. It knew I would procrastinate for years, possibly centuries. About three months ago I started to get some of my print books up. Guess what?

Yes, I started having sales.

Hey Brian, did you do all of your books then?

No, of course not. Hot mess…remember? [Honorée here: I've been telling Brian for *quite some time* that paperback versions of his books would be a great idea. Just sayin'.]

The third book in my Magellan Apocalypse series just needs the cover done to be ready. It would take me an hour. Still not done.

But it gets worse. As I write this, the sequel to *Underwood, Scotch, and Wry* (*Underwood, Scotch and Cry)* is completely done, cover and all. I literally just need to upload it, and the book will be finished. Maybe ten more minutes. Heck, I've already done the ISBN stuff and everything. Just need to upload.

It's been in a holding pattern for over two months.

Honorée here: As of the final review of this book, January 24, 2017, I am happy to report that *US&C* has been published in ebook form and currently has 34 reviews. Please send Brian some encouragement so he finishes the print version in the very near future. Or, before 2027. Thank you.

Back to Brian.

I've found great advertising strategies that make me a bundle of money. For those, I generally do a fine job, but I could list half a dozen things I could do better. Most of them wouldn't take too much time.

Okay, the worst of the blunders has been building my mailing list. This is one of the most important things an author should do. And it should be a focus from day one.

I'm still not great at it.

With every launch, I'm missing out on opportunities because I've not given list building enough attention.

There are more stories, so many stories, but I'm guessing you get the point. You don't need to be perfect to be successful. You don't even need to be exceptional. You just need to pick a few battles and go after them with a vengeance. You'll be fine.

10

THE BEST OFFENSE IS A GOOD DEFENSE

The goal of this book is to help you improve your business and make more money. The goal of this chapter is to keep you from losing years of work by doing something stupid.

Do you know what the most idiotic thing is that one can do in this business?

It has the power to destroy *all* the books you have published.

Unless you've seen this blunder in action, you can't appreciate how quickly things can go south for an author. I mean a rocket-propelled descent into review hell.

The blunder is the rebuttal to a negative review.

The day will come where someone doesn't like your book. It will happen. Doubt me? Go check out your favorite author and read their one-star reviews. The bad review still stings, and I've had plenty. But I never respond unless it is to thank them for their honest review and to say I'm sorry they didn't enjoy my book. Sometimes I even offer another title if they want to send me an email.

I never argue with their reason for writing the review.

This blunder has many forms. Sometimes it starts with something as simple as writing something stupid that pisses off a demographic who is fiercely loyal to another author.

Over a year ago, a woman (whom I won't name) wrote a blog post suggesting that J.K. Rowling should stop writing and give other authors a chance. I read it about an hour after it was posted and shook my head. She was in trouble.

I'm a Harry Potter fan, but that's not what upset me. It's the logic that this woman thought her books were suffering because of one other author's work. That's just ridiculous. Harry Potter fans read lots of books.

This woman wrote literary fiction, was traditionally published, and had several books out. All of them had 3.8 to 4.0 averages on a few hundred reviews each.

What do you think happened when the fiercely loyal Harry Potter fans started to leave comments on her blog?

She started to argue with them. Poorly. This just made them more upset.

If you learn only one thing from this book, it should be this: *Your book is an easy target!*

Within a few hours, her best book had received about ten one-star reviews. The average had dropped to 3.2. None of these people had read her book. They had read the stupid blog post.

If you think Amazon will take down those reviews, you'd be wrong.

I went back a few days later, and all of her books were now below 2.8 average. The reviews were nasty. They were mean. And I doubt her publisher was thrilled that she had destroyed the reputation of all of her works. Also, I noticed the overall ranking of these books had dropped markedly during that time. Yes, sales dried up.

If you keep your eyes open, you'll see one of these stupid blog battles once or twice a year, and the author that tries to defend their work *always* loses.

The author that has thin skin is like a wounded baby gazelle in the open Serengeti. The blog trolls get one whiff of blood, and they descend like a pack of jackals.

Do you want to be eaten by jackals?

I didn't think so.

Yes, it's painful to have someone call your baby ugly, but you need to find a way to cope.

Me, I have an excellent way to deal with the stinging wound. I go to Amazon, look up *A Farewell to Arms*, by Ernest Hemingway, and read those one-star reviews. They are brutal and make me happy.

"Ignore the trolls" is more than just another rule. This is the golden rule of author survival.

Ignoring those that leave bad reviews and not leaving yourself open to unnecessary criticism means you don't want to blather on about politics, either. Go ahead and think of a politician or political pundit who has written a book. It doesn't matter if it is from the red states or the blue states, you'll find reviews from the opposing view by people who live to rant about how wrong they are. Those people can just as easily turn on your book.

When you see a meme that drives you nuts, and the brilliant reply jumps into your head, look away! Do not do it!

Ask yourself, "Am I willing to risk *everything* I've worked for to write a rebuttal that won't convince the reviewer of anything?"

The answer is no.

11

WHAT CONSTITUTES "NOTEWORTHY" IN DATA?

B rian here.

You might be wondering how you can tell the difference between noteworthy data and data that doesn't truly matter? Answer: anything, including data, is noteworthy if it makes you pause and ask a question.

I was planning some Facebook advertising for Honorée's book, *The Divorced Phoenix*, and needed to come up with a solid plan for targeting the ads. This chapter is about the thought process that went into finding my targets. The first thing I did was ask Google for information about divorce rates. I wanted to know if it varied by region or state.

I also wanted to know an age range that represented when the largest group of women get divorced, and as such, might just be looking for a book to help them through the aftermath.

Before I found the numbers I was looking for, I ran across something interesting that I filed away in my notes. January is considered divorce month. I also learned that the divorce rate among people over fifty has doubled in the past twenty years. Again, it was added to my notes.

Forty-eight percent of people who get married before age eighteen are likely to get divorced. That's interesting, but not exactly what I was looking for, so I kept digging.

I kept reading and spotted a paradox. Political affiliation matters in the divorce rate, with conservatives getting divorced twenty-eight percent of the time vs. liberals at thirty-seven percent. Shortly after that, I noticed that the five states with the highest divorce rate were all considered red (conservative) states.

Why is it that the highest divorce rates are in states filled with conservatives, who have the lowest divorce rate? Or, conversely, why do blue states have the lowest divorce rates when they are filled with liberals, who have the highest divorce rate?

There must be an answer to explain the paradox. It was evident that finding the answer would dramatically influence my decisions regarding how I approached the ads for Honorée's book.

The answer was interesting. I won't bore you with all the details, but in short, conservative women get married at a younger age than liberal women. Twenty-eight percent of them will get divorced and then remarry. The chance of divorce dramatically increases with each successive marriage. Their counterparts in the blue states waited longer to get married, and though a greater percentage of the women will get divorced they will stay in the marriage much longer.

What is happening is that in the red states the number of divorces is made up of people who are not just getting divorced, they're getting divorced more than once. So, that's how red states have a higher divorce rate than blue states while liberals have a higher divorce rate than conservatives.

The key for the advertising was in knowing the age ranges that would be most likely to need a book like Honorée's and to plan accordingly. The better the targeting, the greater the chance the person seeing the ad will need what it is you offer.

We are trying to train you to look for things that seem odd and then to dig deeper until the truth is revealed. Also, prior to doing any marketing or advertising, it is important to do market research and look for obvious facts and trends that can influence which direction or approach to take.

12

KEYWORDS "FOR THE WIN!"

S o, we've finally got you convinced, and you're
ready to analyze something, anything. First
things first, my friend. Keywords aren't
individual words, per se. They are "word strings," or
"word phrases." Although you can use just one word
as your keyword, we would advise against it. Here's
why.

Keywords are the little sections on the KDP, CreateSpace, and ACX dashboards, consisting of up to seven keywords, designed to help Amazon know who might like your book.

When a reader is looking for a new title, and while they don't have a specific title in mind, they have a genre or topic in mind. They do a search on Amazon (or the other venues). A fan of mystery novels might type "mystery." They might want a specific type of mystery and type "private detective mystery." It's also possible they don't know what type of mystery they want, will start typing "mystery," and then see that Amazon has some suggestions for them: "mystery and suspense," "mystery books," "mystery thriller suspense," and about eight more. Try it yourself: type in "mystery" in the search box and see what else Amazon serves up to you in the drop-down box. We tried it, and got: "mystery books," "mystery best sellers," "mystery books for kids 9-12," "mystery and thrillers," "mystery novels," "mystery mosaics," and "mystery and suspense."

These prospective readers are free to click on any of those keywords, and Amazon will deliver a unique list of books for their reading pleasure.

These readers are wonderful. They are what we call "organic traffic." This is a reader who doesn't know anything about you, but if they should stumble across your book, might give it a try. If enough people do that, you start to build a following that expands the scope of your reach.

Think about this for a moment. If a friend from high school reads your book and shares how much they loved it on Facebook, there will be some of their followers who are already in your circle of influence because you both know each other from high school.

Now, consider an organic reader who lives in 2,340 miles from you and has never heard of your book. If they give it a try and then share it with their friends, you're reaching a whole new group of possible readers (think potentially hundreds, thousands, or tens of thousands of new readers), who are also organic.

The bottom line is: *we love organic readers.* Organic readers are just what an author needs to encourage word-of-mouth, to sell more books, and ultimately (and this is our favorite part), earn a living from their writing.

To help these precious folks find your book, you need to craft killer keywords.

There are some valuable pieces of information to consider as you begin to make your list of keyword candidates.

- Number of books in a keyword search
- Success of books on the first page of that search (ranking)

- Price of books on the first page of the search
- Accuracy of the keyword as it pertains to your title.

LET'S LOOK AT THE FIRST BULLET POINT: NUMBER OF BOOKS IN A KEYWORD SEARCH.

Before you do a search, it's best to tell the search bar that you want to limit your search to "Kindle Store." The rest of the advice and data in this chapter assume you did just that.

To find out the number of books that are associated with a keyword, simply do a search on Amazon. At the time of editing this chapter, the keyword "Mystery" returned 15,660 books available for Kindle. "Mystery and Suspense" has 166,234.

Those are two different size ponds. What I mean is that at different points in your book's life, you'll want it to try to be a big fish in a little pond, then a big fish in a bigger pond, and someday a HUGE fish in the ocean.

An example of a keyword that would be considered a small pond is "whodunit." There are only 1,260 books that are returned in this search.

This is where the term "long tail keyword" comes into play. When we mentioned that you are only allowed seven keywords, that doesn't mean only seven individual words. "Mystery and Suspense" would count as one keyword. Each keyword, regardless of length, is separated by a comma. A long tail keyword is a multiple word phrase that is very specific. While it may not match many books, the odds are good that if a reader uses that keyword phrase, they know exactly what they are looking for.

Our goal is to have our books show up as early in the search as possible. Page one is best, page two is second best, page three is still good, page one hundred and fifty isn't very valuable.

The better the result, the better the chance to get organic readers.

MOVING ON TO BULLET POINT 2: THE SUCCESS OF THE BOOKS ON PAGE ONE.

We use a tool called Kindle Samurai, but before we discovered it, we manually looked at each book on the first page of the search result to see a few books that are selling well. If all the books are ranked 100,000 or worse, then that tells us something.

It only takes one or two sales to crack 100K in the rankings, so if all the books in a search are below that number, then that is telling me that those books haven't had any sales in a day or two. If none of the books in a search are generating sales, it's probably because there aren't that many people using that search term.

Now, conversely, if there are books that are ranked high, meaning one or two in the category also ranks in the top thousand, and the rest between 1,000 and 100,000, then that's a good sign. It isn't the whole truth, though.

You must consider that there are lots of factors that go into a high ranking. The books on the first page of a search term may be getting lots of sales from other search terms, or from ads, or from people hearing about them on podcasts, or...

You get the idea. We can't assume that a good looking first page makes a keyword term great with only one data point, but we can decide that the keyword is worth adding to our candidate list.

BULLET 3: THE PRICE OF THE BOOKS ON THE FIRST PAGE.

It's easy to get fooled because of "perma-free" books (books that are "permanently free"). If twelve of the sixteen books on page one are free, you'll need to consider whether you want your book that is priced at $4.99 to be competing with all the others priced at zero. It may be a good strategy. There might be people who've grown tired of free books, and so yours will stand out. Brian doesn't have any data on this subject but does know he avoids these search terms (as does Honorée). You'll need to decide for yourself.

There is also the opposite, where a lot of the books are priced at $12.99 or higher. These are typically traditionally published books. There are a lot of people who refuse to buy a book priced over $9.99, so if you can land your book in among these titles, it may give you a huge competitive advantage.

Tip: Sophisticated authors use a strategy called "first free book in a series" to entice new readers to try their books. If readers of the first book like it, the assumption is they will go on to buy and read the rest of the books in the series. This is the "read-through rate" we talked about earlier, and a good read-through rate means you've got a good chance of making a living from your books.

Finally … Bullet Point 4: Accuracy of the Keyword.

If you spend any time wading through search results on Amazon, you'll notice books that just don't belong. If a person is looking for a cozy mystery, they're unlikely to choose something that looks out of place and instead go with a vampire slasher title.

Yes, it's true that people read many different genres, but we must think in terms of large numbers and build our strategies around that which will give us the best chance with the most people.

Remember, keyword accuracy is important.

Furthermore, if you fudge just a little, and get a sale because of it, but the person wanted hard-boiled mystery, and you delivered a cozy mystery instead, then it may well lead to the dreaded one-star review.

So, now that you have a basic understanding, let's build a keyword list.

Brian is the master here, so let's let him take it away:

Step One: Build Your List of Keywords

1. Open a blank Excel workbook.
2. Click on the tab and change "Sheet 1" to "Keywords."
3. Save your workbook as something like "Keyword Master List to Dominate the World."
4. Now, in the first row put a header. If you have more than one book, it might be good to have the first column labeled "Book title." Make the second column "Keyword."

Since this is the first foray into data analysis, I think I should mention a couple of things I *always* do.

If I'm gathering data that I will revisit and take another sampling, like we're about to do with keywords, then I always include a date stamp in another column.

Then, I try to anticipate future needs for my data.

- Possibly use this analysis for a future book in the same genre
- Possibly use the data to write a book on keywords (which I'm doing now. See what I did there?)
- Use my data to support an article or speech

The point is I include the title of the book I'm analyzing because I may need it later. If you write across multiple genres (or even if you don't), time has a way of making the little details fade, so you'll ask yourself, *What was I researching the keyword "Penguin Antics" for?*

Also, if you have date stamps, you can then combine data from one source with another, say, sales or rankings, and do an even deeper analysis.

Okay, let's continue:

5. Write down the first keyword that comes to mind for your book.

6. Go to Amazon and type that word into search but don't hit enter.

7. Look at all the other searches that are suggested (other search terms will automatically appear in the drop-down box). Those are the long tail keywords.

8. Do any of them look good (i.e., do they directly relate to your book)? If yes, go ahead and start copying them into your Excel workbook, adding each one to the Keyword column.

9. Now, take that first keyword and put it back into search. Add a space, then add the letter "a." This will encourage other search terms to populate. Did Amazon give you more long tail suggestions? See any good ones?

10. You can do this for the entire alphabet if you like.

And your first keyword list is off to a roaring start. Don't forget to hit save.

Now, pick a few keywords that look good and highlight them in your list. Go ahead and do a search on Amazon and check out the first page of results. You are about to do some analysis. Are you excited?

- Click on the first book returned.
- What is its rank?
- How many reviews does it have?
- What does the cover look like?
- Did they use the keyword in their title?
- Did they use the keyword in their sub-title?

These are the sorts of questions that are always on my mind. I'm trying to figure out why the book is showing up on the first page.

Okay, now look at the second book. Is there a vast difference in the rank? There probably is because it's not uncommon for a book or two that aren't selling particularly well to show up on page one for a short while. If it starts to sell, it just might stay there.

The point is that right now you're digging into search. The goal is to see the results as the readers do and to become familiar with what is working and what isn't. The more you do it the more likely you'll start to see patterns.

After spending some time on page one, go to page two and look at one or two books. Keep going through the pages for as long as you can, or schedule another time to devote to your research.

I know, that sounds awful, but it is amazing how much I've learned by sometimes looking at 150 pages of a single search. And then doing it again for the next search term.

In fact, I've become familiar with a lot of books that are competing with mine for the same eyeballs.

There was one author who I'd seen so much I knew what his books are generally ranked. One day I saw his book and checked it, as I so often do, and it was *way* up the charts. I mean, super high, higher than I'd ever seen it before.

The question becomes, *how did that happen?*

My first guess was that he must have a BookBub ad. I went to my inbox and checked. There was the day's BookBub email blast. I opened it, and sure enough, there was his book, priced 99 cents.

You'd be amazed at how often I'm able to make educated guesses about something and be right. It isn't that I've got some special superpower (as far as you know), it's that I'm so familiar with the norm and what it takes to make a change, I'm able to create a hypothesis where others would be just chalking it up to "luck."

Back to the keywords.

I spend hours and hours doing what I described above. It's the sort of thing one can do casually while sports drone on in the background. College football is ideal for research because there's a lot of time between plays and a billion commercials. It makes the research less like work and more like just a thing I'm doing.

Of course, if you don't watch college football, then there isn't anything you can do. You're doomed. Give up.

Not really, but if you cheer for the Ohio State Buckeyes, I'm sure it will help your results. I digress.

STEP TWO: NARROW DOWN YOUR LIST OF KEYWORDS

After spending some time in the search results of your keywords, you've likely found a few that are easy to eliminate. That's good.

Note: It's best to add a column next to the keyword column and indicate "yes" or "no" for each keyword as you analyze it. Most people would just delete the ones they've eliminated. The problem with that approach is that in six months, when you write another book and go back to your list, you won't likely remember the ones you got rid of. You'll run the risk of needing to reanalyze them again. That's wasted time. Always keep your data, even if the answer is "not a chance."

Now, let's dig deeper.

Go back to the first keyword that remains with a "yes" by it. Put it back into search, and in the column to the right of the "yes," type in the number of books in the category.

As I mentioned before, we now use a tool called Samurai Kindle. I like it, but I'm not saying it's 100% necessary. What it allows me to do is put in a search term, and then it scrapes the first page of the search and returns more data. It gives the number of books that have listed the keyword in the title and description. It tells the best-ranked book, the lowest ranking book, the average rank, number of reviews, average price, and there is a "conclusion" column which seems to be based upon the number of books in the keyword search. Often it reads "very difficult."

The tool isn't perfect. The average price is often skewed by free books. Sometimes it doesn't find the rank of a book. Amazon is constantly updating and changing their site to make it better. This means that they may have rolled out a new page design for some books as a test. As such, the scraping program isn't finding all the data for those books.

With this in mind, I can't recommend you get Samurai Kindle because I don't know how effective the tool will be when you are reading this chapter. Personally, I do like it and hope that it is kept in good working order, but I have no way of knowing what the future might hold.

So, you could manually calculate those metrics, which even a data lover like me thinks would be dreadful, or you could come up with some of your own. You might decide to scan the first page and look at the stuff one can easily see, like price and number of reviews. You could have a column that is simply "good" or "bad" to indicate how you felt those pieces looked to you on the whole.

Is that as good as exact data? No, but as I mentioned even the tool I use isn't exact. A "good or bad" rating like I referred to above is still really valuable. The more you use a system, too, the better you'll get at seeing patterns.

STEP THREE: CATEGORIZING YOUR KEYWORDS

Below is the breakdown I use for categorizing the number of books returned by each keyword search. You may use mine or create your own. I had reasons for this chart, but you may have better reasons to adjust it for your own use. The important thing is to stick with whatever you choose for future analysis.

- Puddle = 0 – 2000
- Pond = 2001 – 5000
- Lake = 5001 – 10000
- Reservoir = 10001 – 25000
- Bay = 25001 – 50000
- Ocean. = 50001 – A Gazillion (I use 1.3 million)

You can simply reference the chart and then, in a new column, put in the body of water.

If you are feeling extra motivated or are familiar with the "VLookup" function in Excel, you'll be able to create the chart in Excel and then write a formula to reference it. That's what I do. VLookup is a powerful function, and if you spend the time to figure it out, you'll be able to use it a lot in your analysis.

The other beautiful thing about a look-up chart is that if you should ever decide to alter the count ranges, you can do so, and the new body of water will be updated on all of your research. You may decide my ranges suck and want to use your own. If you do a chart, you'll have that option without having to go back and review all your keywords again.

STEP FOUR: MAKING SOME DECISIONS

You've built a nice little chunk of data, and now it's time to analyze it. This is the fun part. I'm talking "eating bacon at an amusement park" level of fun.

Do you want to be a big fish in a puddle or go for the Ocean?

The puddle will have less traffic. The Ocean will be hard for your book to get to the top.

Here are some things I've learned as I have worked with my own keywords over the last year. I started with a mix of the smaller bodies of water. The idea was to see if I could get my book showing up in the search results and then, when I succeeded (as I'm always sure I will), to change my keywords and try to move up to a bigger body of water.

It sort of worked. It sort of failed.

What we haven't talked about are all the ways keywords help your book. We will do that in the next chapter. Right now, let me tell you what I found with my own research.

There are a lot of people trying the big fish little pond method. What I'm not seeing, though, is that once they've crushed it in the smaller bodies of water, that they're now revisiting their keywords and trying to move into a lake or ocean.

This means that there are a whole lot of authors who are going after long tail keywords that have less competition. At least, on the surface they appear to have less competition because of the book count. The truth is that some of these puddles and ponds are as hard to crack as the larger search terms.

I've changed my focus to larger bodies of water and am having reasonable success. As of the writing of this chapter, October 2016, my satire, *Underwood, Scotch, and Wry* shows up on page 2 row 3 of "Humor and Satire." There are 23,354 books in this search. It's been on page two for over two months. Also, during that time, *Underwood, Scotch, and Wry* has been ranked between #521 and #2000 overall for nearly the entire time.

Is it all because of that one term? No. I do a lot of marketing, but I can tell you that I do get organic sales, and I'm sure some of them find me under "Humor and Satire."

Important Note: Not all searches are the same. If you do a search and find your book on page 1 row 8, then you get excited and call your cousin in Texas and have them do the search, they may find your book on page 3 row 9. The algorithm is complex. There may be a regional component. There may be a bias because you search for your book so often that Amazon knows this.

What I do know is that a book doing well in a term when you search is going to still do reasonably well (sometimes better) when another person does the search. So, don't be disappointed if your friend doesn't get the exact same result.

It should also be noted that when a book like this one mentions a strategy like going for a larger pond, if lots of people have read this book, that will dampen the effectiveness. If the people who had been in the puddles suddenly start splashing around in the lakes, then you may want to move again.

The way I get a sense of who is playing where is the price. If there are lots of 99 cent and free books, those are the hallmarks of beginning Indie authors.

Once you become more established you'll find it beneficial to charge more (not just financially, but because it puts your book in a better class).

WHICH BRINGS US TO STEP FIVE: REVIEW!

It's probably not what you wanted to hear, but this may be the most important step. It's one I dreaded doing at first until I started to see some real blunders with my keywords. You need to go back and review your keywords on a regular basis.

I'm going through the review of all fourteen of my published titles and a few of Honorée's titles as well. In almost every book, I'm finding one to three keywords that are just not doing anything for me. I'm not finding my book in the top 100 results pages, so I might as well try a keyword that gets better traction.

The review process will also give you a new set of data. If you used Kindle Samurai and saved each of the searches, like I do, and then dumped them into a spreadsheet, then you'll be able to compare the state of the first page vs. what it was the last time you did the analysis.

Imagine a book is still on page one after a three-month period. *That* is a book I want to watch. I want to read their description and look for the keywords they've included. I want to see if I can find the other keywords they've used and where they rank. This author is doing it right so let's see if we can find out why.

On the other hand, what if a book that was page one, row four, is now on page fifteen, row twelve. What happened?

It will be hard to know for sure, but like everything, the more you get in the practice of asking those questions, the more likely you'll see things that others miss.

Example: At the beginning of the year, I noticed a change at Amazon that seemed to be impacting my number of sales. I had a theory that it was something that would correct itself and predicted to Honorée that around the first week in February, the problem would fade.

I was right, and by the second week in February, my sales were back where I expected. There wasn't anything I could do about it but by having a theory as to why it was happening, I didn't lose any sleep until I knew if I was right or not. If I had been wrong, well, I would have needed to formulate a new plan. Thankfully, I wasn't.

What's Next?

You've settled on your seven keywords and entered them into your book's metadata (on page one of your KDP book details page). Are you done?

Nope.

Amazon is a search engine. That means they are looking for all the information possible to deliver to the screen what the customer is most likely to buy.

This means that the wording in your description may also come into play. If you use the word "mystery" as one of your keywords, why not work that into the description?

You don't want to stuff keywords, though. It might make the copywriting less effective. This would be bad. *Very bad.*

If you have a choice between writing, "You'll enjoy this novel" or "You'll enjoy this mystery novel," go with the second one. You may also start showing up in the keyword "mystery novel," even though it wasn't one of the ones you chose.

Yes, it is possible to show up in searches you didn't expect. Also, it's possible to have a keyword and not show up at all.

I did a test with a keyword that was in a puddle. It was small enough that after the search I went through all of the pages that were returned. You guessed it. My book, despite having that keyword, didn't show up at all.

Conversely, I was researching the massive category Literature and Fiction, which I wasn't using as a keyword on any of my books. Sure enough, Killing Hemingway was on page 150. If you consider there are sixteen books per page, that means that Killing Hemingway was in the top 2,400 of a category that has 1.2 million books in it, and I didn't even have it selected as one of my keywords.

So, how did it get there?

Well, there is another important search component. In step 3 of your book's KDP set-up, you are asked to provide two categories. I had chosen "FICTION>Coming of Age" and "FICTION> Literary."

I didn't even remember doing it, but that is likely the reason *Killing Hemingway* is showing up.

Now, admittedly, being on page 150 isn't generating me any sales, but what if I added it to my keyword list in place of one of the ones that wasn't helping?

What if I worked it into my description?

These are the questions I'm always asking myself, and one of them is how I come up with test ideas. I don't know if I'll ever be able to get *Killing Hemingway* on one of the first few pages of Literature and Fiction, but it's worth a try. And if I do, it will be worth a few sales.

Have you ever noticed how some people include ": A Novel" in their title? *The Girl with the Guinea Pig Tattoo: A Novel.* Well, you can bet they did it to help with the keywords. It's the same with sub-titles. This is another thing to keep an eye out for on books that seem to be on the first few pages of the search, did they include a term in the title?

My book, *Henry Wood Detective Agency,* always does well in the "detective" related searches. I wasn't a genius, though, in planning the title. That's just what I called my book when I started writing it years before I even knew I would finish or publish. I did add the subtitle *"Henry Wood Detective Series Book 1"* as a subtitle.

The rule of thumb is this: Amazon is fine with subtitle if they are A) on the cover or B) an accurate representation of the book. Amazon doesn't want you misrepresenting your book, though, so please try to be accurate.

DOUBLE SECRET KEYWORD IDEA...

Yes, that was an Animal House reference. Amazon doesn't tell us how their search engine works, so it's up to us to do our best to make the hypothesis and then look for correlations that would give us a reasonable confidence that they're true. We'll never be able to see behind the curtain and prove our results. And the magic behind the curtain will change periodically. But if we have a solid understanding, we'll have an advantage over the rest of the authors.

It seems reasonable then that Amazon may look at the reviews that are left by readers. This made me wonder if I could reply to the reviews and use a certain keyword to help my results.

I tested the theory several times. I can say with confidence that my replies had zero effect. It would be too easy to game if it did, but I still wanted to know for sure.

It does seem like the words people use in their reviews can impact search results. This goes back to what I was discussing with showing up for search terms which I didn't choose.

How is that helpful, Brian? We're not writing the reviews.

True, you don't control what goes into the review, but you do control what's in the title of your book. How many people mention the title when writing a review?

And then here is the secret idea part. When you're reading the reviews, keep an eye open for descriptive terms that keep showing up. If you've never thought of your book as literature, but three people use that term, then maybe you need to do some research and see if you should put it in your keywords.

13

YOU'VE GOT MORE ANALYTICAL EXPERIENCE THAN YOU THINK

I t's a Saturday afternoon.

The husband sits down at the kitchen table and takes out his new purchase from the Apple Store. The wife smiles at his childlike joy as she reviews some work reports sent over by mergers and acquisitions.

For a moment, they are both content. He's got his new toy, and the project she's been working on looks like it's a go. The husband looks up at his lovely wife and says, "Are the kids outside playing? It's nice to have some quiet."

The wife looks up from her laptop. Her expression changes. She doesn't move. It's quiet. Too quiet.

"No."

"You mean…" Husband says with a look of fear in his eyes.

"Yes, the quiet, it's coming from inside the house."

Parents know that children of a certain age have only two modes, trouble and plotting trouble, the second of which can lead to destruction most aptly described as thorough, bordering on post-hurricane. Few people survive.

One doesn't need to have formal training as a data analyst to think like one. Your subconscious is constantly seeing patterns and figuring out solutions. The best route to work, the easiest way to get to dance practice and soccer, the rule to never go to the amusement park on the Fourth of July weekend, are but a few of the hundreds of examples of analysis your brain has done without you even trying.

You've got this. We know this because you now have an understanding of math and the other numbers you can use in your favor, and how awesome they can all be! Becoming a successful, prosperous, and full-time writer is essentially as simple as understanding the numbers, and making the numbers work for you.

While easier said than done, when becoming a writer possesses every cell of your being, is all you can think about, and your dream is to make a living from your writing, what other choice do you have but to figure it out? Your other option is to give up, and frankly, we don't think that's much of an option at all. We would commend you if we would take our advice and implement it immediately because that's how convinced we are our advice will work for you. But that would be rude, and we are not rude. So instead we heartily encourage you to heed our advice. To become the writer you've always dreamed of being, to fully understand how to make your numbers work for you, and to share your talents and gifts with the world. And, we hope you'll tell us all about it!

Now go forth and calculate and write!

Resources

LINKS TO OTHER BOOKS IN THE PROSPEROUS WRITERS SERIES:

Prosperity for Writers: A Writer's Guide to Creating Abundance
(The Prosperous Writer Series Book 1)
http://tinyurl.com/ProsperityforWriters

Prosperity for Writers Productivity Journal: A Writer's Workbook for Creating Abundance
http://tinyurl.com/P4WJournal

The Nifty 15: Write Your Book in Just 15 Minutes a Day
(The Prosperous Writer Series Book 2)
http://tinyurl.com/Nifty15

144

LINKS TO OUR NEWSLETTERS AND OTHER AWESOMESAUCENESS:

The Prosperous Writer Mastermind:
HonoreeCorder.com/Writers

***The Prosperous Writer's Guide to Making More Money* Bonuses:**
HonoreeCorder.com/M3Bonuses

BEST BOOK BUSINESS READS:

On Writing: A Memoir of the Craft (Stephen King)
http://tinyurl.com/SKingOnWriting

Your First 1000 Copies: The Step-by-Step Guide to Marketing Your Book (Tim Grahl)
http://tinyurl.com/First1000Copies

You Must Write a Book: Boost Your Brand, Get More Business, and Become the Go-To Expert (Honorée Corder)
http://tinyurl.com/YouMustWriteaBook

The Miracle Morning for Writers: How to Build a Writing Ritual That Increases Your Impact and Your Income (Hal Elrod & Steve Scott, with Honorée Corder)
http://tinyurl.com/MM4Writers

WRITING AND SELF-PUBLISHING PODCASTS TO LISTEN TO:

Authors' note: There are so many great podcasts, this is not the full list, just a few of our favorites to get you started.

The Author Biz Podcast
TheAuthorBiz.com

The Author Hangout
BookMarketingTools.com/blog

The Self-Publishing Podcast
SterlingandStone.net/podcasts

The Sell More Books Show
SellMoreBooksShow.com

The Smarty Pants Book Marketing Podcast
SmartyPantsBookMarketing.libsyn.com/podcast

The Wordslinger Podcast
KevinTumlinson.com/podcast-rss

The Writer Files Podcast
Rainmaker.fm

Quick Favor

We're wondering, did you enjoy this book?

First of all, thank you for reading our book! May we ask a quick favor?

Will you take a moment to leave an honest review for this book on Amazon? Reviews are the BEST way to help others purchase the book.

You can go to the link below and write your thoughts. We appreciate you!

HonoreeCorder.com/M3Review

ABOUT THE AUTHORS

HONORÉE CORDER is the author of dozens of books, including *You Must Write a Book, Vision to Reality, Prosperity for Writers, Business Dating, The Successful Single Mom* book series, *If Divorce is a Game, These are the Rules,* and *The Divorced Phoenix.* She is also Hal Elrod's business partner in *The Miracle Morning* book series. Honorée coaches business professionals, writers, and aspiring non-fiction authors who want to publish their books to bestseller status, create a platform, and develop multiple streams of income. She also does all sorts of other magical things, and her badassery is legendary. You can find out more at HonoreeCorder.com.

BRIAN D. MEEKS is a full-time author who resides in Iowa when he's not traveling. He writes across mystery, thriller, YA, science fiction, and humor/satire fiction genres. He has a degree in Economics from Iowa State University only because they didn't offer Snarkology, his preferred major. Seven years as a data analyst in the auto insurance industry gave him the skills that have been key to his success in marketing his books and finding an audience. He really likes it when people send him pictures of their cats or guinea pigs.

THE PROSPEROUS WRITER BOOK SERIES

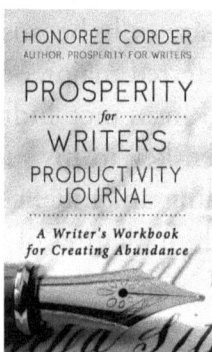

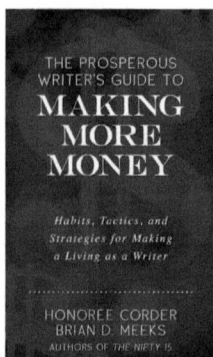

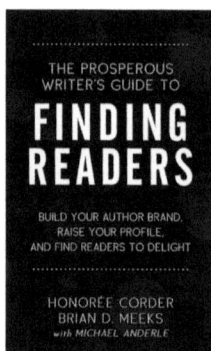

PROSPERITY
···· *for* ····
WRITERS

*A Writer's Guide
to Creating Abundance*

HONORÉE CORDER
AUTHOR OF VISION TO REALITY

HONORÉE CORDER
AUTHOR, PROSPERITY FOR WRITERS

PROSPERITY
for
WRITERS
PRODUCTIVITY
JOURNAL

*A Writer's Workbook
for Creating Abundance*

THE PROSPEROUS WRITER SERIES

THE NIFTY

15

*Write Your Book in Just
15 Minutes a Day!*

HONORÉE CORDER
AUTHOR, PROSPERITY FOR WRITERS
& BRIAN D. MEEKS

THE PROSPEROUS
WRITER'S GUIDE TO
**MAKING
MORE
MONEY**

*Habits, Tactics, and
Strategies for Making
a Living as a Writer*

HONORÉE CORDER
BRIAN D. MEEKS
AUTHORS OF THE NIFTY 15

THE PROSPEROUS
WRITER'S GUIDE TO
**FINDING
READERS**

BUILD YOUR AUTHOR BRAND,
RAISE YOUR PROFILE,
AND FIND READERS TO DELIGHT

HONORÉE CORDER
BRIAN D. MEEKS
with MICHAEL ANDERLE

COMING SOON ...

The Prosperous Writer's Guide to Mindset

www.ingramcontent.com/pod-product-compliance
Lightning Source LLC
Chambersburg PA
CBHW070839300326
41935CB00038B/1145